"*Here's My Heart* is
heart-felt, soul-stirring
reading. Ray Hardin's magnificent use of language to create breathtaking images, ignite the imagination, and stir the emotions sets this work apart as a collection of prayers. From beginning to end, *Here's My Heart* offers unforgettable prayers of praise and of lament from the dusk of an admirable life journey."

—**Timothy Spivey**, Lead Minister, New Vintage Church, San Diego, California

"Within non-liturgical churches there is a widespread misunderstanding of the value of written prayers. Because of this shortsighted bias against the sincerity and value of anything but the spontaneous, our worship and spiritual life is deprived of a rich source of blessing from prayers which are thought out deeply and expressed richly. Into this void, steps Ray Hardin. He has written a helpful contemporary book of psalms which can focus our minds and enrich our spirits. This refreshing volume would be a great addition to the library of any believer but especially for those who lead worship."

—**Dan Bouchelle**, Executive Director of Missions Resource Network

"The reading of Ray Hardin's prayers feels like experiencing King David supplying a contemporary addendum to his collection of Psalms. These words are a refreshing expression of honesty and transparency combined with spiritual depth and wisdom."

—**Curtis Williams**, Preaching Minister, North Pointe Church of Christ, Murphy, Texas

"Poems express what prose and pronouncements cannot. Poets dwell in deep places, accessible only through portals of life-pain, joy, meditation, and solitude. Ray Hardin's written prayers—poems to God, for God, and for us—simultaneously translate his heart, our hearts, and God's heart through rare, transparent, and poignant language. Ray's prayer-poems illuminate my continual, desperate need for deep, relational conversation with God."

—**Jon Mullican**, Executive Minister, Highland Oaks Church of Christ, Dallas, Texas - Plano, Texas

"Ray Hardin has held nothing back in *Here's My Heart*. Through highly personal prayers, using simple, natural, honest language, Ray offers a way to access our deepest and most complex thoughts about our lives and our relationship with God. This book will urge you to drink deeply from the spiritual waters and will stir within you a longing for the Lord."

—**Rick Gibson**, Chief Marketing Officer, Pepperdine University

"I've never been very good at prayer. Silent prayer leaves my mind wandering and my spoken prayers often circle back around to meaningless clichés and self-centered requests. In this collection of prayers, like the psalmists, Ray Hardin models for me a way to pray deep, thoughtful prayers that express the doubts and desires of my heart in a way that keeps me tethered to the immense love of God."

—**Wade Hodges**, author of *Before You Go: A Few Sneaky Good Questions for Ministers*

"Ray Hardin's heart has long been turned toward God. His prayers have long blessed his church, his friends in ministry and leadership, and legions of those who have known challenges similar to his own. In *Here's My Heart*, Ray gets honest and bold with his faith. Yet his heart is even more hopeful and, yes, joyful. His prayers are what prayers should be. And they help me find words to share my heart with God, too. They will bless you."

—**Charles Siburt**, Frazer Professor of Church Enrichment, Abilene Christian University

"I am so happy that Ray is sharing a second inspiring book of prayers. The fact that he made this project a priority when time is so precious makes this work even more important. His prayers are beautifully worded. But they are special to me because I know they were born out of his love for the Highland Oaks Church and unnumbered individuals whom he has counseled, taught, and encouraged. Each prayer was inspired by real-world needs for specific individuals in particular circumstances. His heart is totally transparent which makes each page a treasure for all who know him and love him. I'm thankful he is my friend."

—**Don Crisp**, Dallas, Texas

"Life greets us in different ways each day. We experience joy and sadness, anticipation and doubt, grief and pain. We walk through seasons of loneliness and times of closeness with God, family, and friends. Each event in our lives, whether big or small, can be an occasion for prayer. In *Here's My Heart*, Ray Hardin shares the prayers he has prayed in moments like these, baring his soul with a medley of honest and open-hearted conversations with God. As you will quickly learn, Ray is a man of God, a passionate follower of Jesus, and an encourager to many. I invite you to pray along with him, expressing your hopes and heartaches to the God who listens."

—**Barry Packer**, Chairman, Board of Trustees, Abilene Christian University

Here's My HEART

James Teague
400 Sheffield Dr
Richardson TX 75081-5540

Here's My HEART

PRAYERS

Ray Hardin

All proceeds from the sale of this book will go to the Raymond L. Hardin Endowment for Church Leadership, which is dedicated to training and equipping mature and effective church leaders.

*Overseen and administered by Highland Oaks Church of Christ
10805 Walnut Hill Drive, Dallas, Texas 75238*

HERE'S MY HEART
Prayers

Copyright 2011 by Ray Hardin

ISBN 978-089112-115-2

Printed in the United States of America

ALL RIGHTS RESERVED
No part of this publication may be reproduced, stored in a retrieval system, or transmitted in any form by any means—electronic, mechanical, photocopying, recording or otherwise—without prior written consent.

Scripture quotations, unless otherwise noted, are from The Holy Bible, New International Version. Copyright 1984, International Bible Society. Used by permission of Zondervan Publishers.

Cover design by Rick Gibson

Leafwood Publishers
1626 Campus Court
Abilene, Texas 79601
1-877-816-4455 toll free

For current information about all Leafwood titles, visit our Web site:
www.leafwoodpublishers.com

For Chris, Misty and Kelly
who have blessed my life through all these years.

Prayer

Prayer, the Church's banquet, Angels' age,
God's breath in man returning to his birth,
The soul in paraphrase, heart in pilgrimage,
The Christian plummet sounding heaven and earth,
Engine against the Almighty, sinners' tower,
Reversed thunder, Christ-side piercing-spear,
The six-days world-transposing in an hour,
A kind of tune, which all things hear and fear;
Softness, and peace, and joy, and love, and bliss,
Exalted Manna, gladness of the best,
Heaven in ordinary, man well dressed,
The milky way, the bird of Paradise,
Church-bells beyond the stars heard, the soul's blood,
The land of spices something understood.

George Herbert (1593-1633)

CONTENTS

LITTLE PRAYERS

Once for All	21
Radiance	21
Strength and Life	22
Very Early Morning	22
Mend	23
Dear Life	23
Your Name	24
Grateful Heart	24
Waiting for Me	25
Divine Seeds	25
Talking	26
Your Will	26
Maker and Keeper	27
Your Presence	27
Great Love	28
Loving Call	28
Lead Me	29
Stop Running	29
Not Cleaned Up	30
Practice Forgiveness	30
Light of Truth	31
Faithful	31
Abundance	32
Hard Cases	32

OCCASIONS

Just Enough	35
Change Agents	37
for Andrea and Alan	39
Three in One	40
We Need You Now	41
Don't Let Go	42
Blessed Art Thou	45
Lucas Waits	46

Ring Into Our Future 47
Breath of God 49
Revive Them Again 51
Prayer for the Church 54
Reunion 57
Rushing In 59
Have it Your Way 61
Nothing in My Hand 63
Unto Us 65
Lord of Lords 66
Call to Worship 68
Breakfast 70
Your Glory 71
Thanksgiving 72
At Year End 74
Ending Well 77
Redeem It All 78

CRYING OUT

I Am the Blind Man 83
The Search 84
What Is It? 86
Looking Good 88
It's the Waiting 89
Heart Surgery 91
Don't Forsake Us 92
Peace on Earth 94
We Didn't Listen 96
Starting Over 99
To Tell You the Truth 102
Our Words 104
Dare We? 105
Cry Out 106
Ever We Ask 107

THANKS

True to Your Word 111
Beyond Good 113

Second Chance 115
I Won't Take Less 117
Where Would We Be? 118
Regress 120

CONFESSION AND FORGIVENESS

We Confess 123
Looks Like Compassion 125
Come Home 126
Feed Us 127
Gentle Shepherd 128
Dirty Little Secrets 129
You Set the Standard 130

TRUST

We Hear You 133
Choices 135
O Sovereign Lord 137
Whenever You're Ready 139
Teach Us To Pray 142
Sing Over Us 146
You Are My Shield 150
Light of the World 154
Praise to the Lord 156
Cultish Tightness 158
Honor 160
You Have Been Good 161
Call My Name 164

OUTWARD

What Are They Doing Here? 169
Blind Eye 170
Who is My Neighbor? 171
Swallow Us, Lord 174
Objects of Honor 176
Spiritual Leverage 177
Whispered Blessing 178
Guarded Looks 179

GOD'S WILL

Did You Mean?	183
More Like You	184
Giving Way	185
Devoted	186
A Prophet's Voice	187
Sweet Will of God	188
One God	190
Intimate Love Letter	191

FOREWORD

If Ray Hardin speaks, I'm going to listen. It's no more complicated than that. I can remember the first time I heard Ray pray publically. His stately presence towered over the church that Sunday morning and his James Earl Jones voice boomed throughout the sanctuary. But it was the grace-filled words that flowed from his mouth that caught my attention. I knew at that instant that for Ray *words matter*. Especially prayer-full words. After all, according to Jesus the words matter because they flow from what is in your heart. And that is precisely the origin of the prayers compiled in this book—Ray's passionate and sincere heart.

Some would characterize the prayers in this book as stunning poetry. And that would be an accurate assessment. Still others might describe them as "occasional" prayers—well constructed petitions that breathe appropriate emotion into those momentous, life-shaping events. Whatever the case, the prayers offered in this beautiful collection are tools: a means for anyone to express and discover the Almighty's mystery, grace, and otherness.

It was the great Thomas Merton who said, "The real purpose of prayer is the exploration of freedom, illumination, and love, in deepening our awareness of our life in Christ." And this is exactly what Ray's prayers do for me. As I read them the first time I knew they weren't just things you flippantly or frivolously say. No, these prayers were sincere expressions of a heart that has been captured by someone and something much greater. And the carefully scripted words are simply a means to an end. And the end is of course God.

So, in praying these words will you find God? Or in these words does God somehow find you? I'll let you decide. In the meantime I hope you drink them all in. And maybe your experience will be like mine: they will create a space for you to be fully present to the one who has always been fully present to you.

And that is the invitation from my mentor, shepherd, and dearest friend—straight from his heart.

Pat Bills
Lead Minister, Highland Oaks Church of Christ
and pastor to Ray Hardin

INTRODUCTION

My first collection of prayers, *Be Our Strength,* came to life due to the encouragement of a few friends and students. Those prayers were prayed over my classes and the church on special occasions. The idea of publishing them never occurred to me. I couldn't imagine they were interesting enough to capture much attention. To my amazement, that little book has traveled far and wide. I've received words of thanks from folks who don't know me and whom I don't know. They say how much they've been helped by reading and re-reading those prayers. Many said almost the same words: those prayers say what I feel but didn't know how to say. And those prayers have, come to find out, been read aloud in a number of churches of all brands. For this generous reception I am genuinely thankful.

    This current collection of prayers were also prayed over my classes, over the church and at other special events in the life of the church and my friends. And this collection has come together because friends, family, and students—flung across the country—have hounded me mercilessly: *Put it together! Get it done!* And here it is at last, having rested on the corner of my desk for quite a long time while I battled cancer. My physicians say I'm losing the battle and that I'm getting this project done in my last days. That's the clinical rendition. We shall see. God is still in charge of my life and my life-span. My faith has not, and I pray it will not, become subject to my disease, and I'm hopeful that these prayers will reflect that faith.

I pray rich blessings on each reader.

Ray Hardin
Dallas, 2011

Little Prayers

Once for All

Lord, most of all today I'm thankful that you went to such drastic extremes to make peace and to patch things up between
you and us. Between your holiness and our human-ness. Between your wisdom and our dullness. Between your universal vision and our myopia. Between your purity and our unclean-ness. Between your majesty and our ruggedness. You patched it all up...once for all. You cleaned us up. You claimed us as your sons and daughters. Grant us the grace to be genuine peace-makers with each other. For this we will need an extra push of courage from you. For your peace-making, for the push we need to be peace-makers, and for all
your gifts we are thankful.

Radiance

Lord, most of all today I'm thankful that you didn't wind up the world and go away. I'm thankful you showed yourself to us in Jesus. Because without him we'd never really know how much you know and understand us. How much you love us. How available you are to us. And how much you want good things for us. How completely open and honest you've been with us. Grant me, and each of us, the grace to be open to you and to each other. Give us the courage to be genuine with you and real with each other so that we may reflect your love and radiance to each other and to all the world.

Strength and Life

Lord, most of all today I'm thankful I am not surrounded by perfect people who have no problems or burdens or disabilities. For then surely I would be embarrassed and afraid to let anyone see me, the real me. And then I would never have friends. And then I might never truly reach your forgiveness and healing because it is most likely, it seems to me, that I will be brought into your presence by someone who loves us both. Grant me Lord the grace to own up to my failures, my weaknesses, my inadequacies and heartaches. My disabilities and my sins so that with all the saints of all times, behind us and before us, I may look to you, and only to you, for salvation, strength and life.

Very Early Morning

Lord, I feel you working in me, getting me ready for the days ahead.
You are restoring my strength and providing harmony in my body.
You are healing my disease and equipping me for the next phase of my being. Whether here as your servant in your earthly kingdom or within the next dimension—closer to you—I know not.
You have calmed my soul and removed my anxiety. My trust in your plan grows hourly. For these great blessings I am unworthy. But thankful.
Blessed be the name of the Lord.

Mend

We live in a broken world, Lord, redeemed by Jesus but not yet made whole for your glory. So we live with sin and sickness, with aging and wearing out, with disease and death and with fear and broken hearts. Mend first, Lord, the tie that binds us to you. Help us to seek you and love you first and best. Help us to trust you most and always. We beg for healing for those in special need through your grace and the brilliance of medicine, one of your great gifts. We ask for angels to linger near them, offering your peace and love in a way they can sense and feel and know. Through it all, Lord, be with us as we learn to praise you in all things, oh giver of life

Dear Life

How hard it seems for us, Lord, to let go some of the ideas and practices that comfort us so much and sustain us so little. How easy it is for us, Lord, to hold on for dear life to almost anything or anyone except you, who alone can provide dear life.
Teach us to let go. Help us,
Oh dear God, to relax in you.
And to love you best.

Your Name

We worship you, O God, and exalt your name above all names. We honor your power above all powers. We praise your goodness above all good. We bless you as our God, the one true, living, caring, sustaining, rescuing and loving God. We confess we are not worthy except through the redemption freely given us by your son Jesus. Thank you for that greatest of all blessings.

Grateful Heart

Lord, I am prone to leave you, to wander off on my own. As if I could really make it on my own. How many times you have showered me with unspeakably rich gifts? How many times you have rescued me from outrageously dangerous circumstances... and from myself? How many times have you provided just the right person or opportunity at just the right time? And how often I have taken it all and run. Help me to give you the credit. Create in me a grateful heart, O God.

Waiting for Me

Lord, when I call out to you and tell you what I need and ask for what I want, I expect you to come through for me...and quick. I don't like being left without answers...without the results I expect. Sometimes I wonder what you are waiting for. And then I think maybe...just maybe...you are waiting for me. Waiting for me to remember and you that you are still and always in control. That you haven't forgotten us. That you know us and want only good for us. That you love us. And that right in the middle of our need, pain, disappointment, loss and apparent hopelessness, you are there for us...our God. *Our help in ages past, our hope for years to come, our shelter from the stormy blast, and our eternal home.*

Divine Seeds

Lord, you know how competitive I am. How I want to win. And be loved. And admired. Help me to stop and go back for those who have fallen. Or are in trouble; those with broken hearts and shattered dreams. Soften my heart, Lord, and plant your divine seeds of compassion within us so we can offer up to you unending prayers for each other.

Talking

How easy it becomes for me to always
be talking, Lord. Sometimes to
others. Sometimes to myself.
Sometimes even to you.
Help me be quiet. To
not talk so much. To learn to
listen to you...to hear your
voice. Speak to me, most
holy God, the most important
things I can hear.

Your Will

How easy it is for me to want what
I want, Lord, When I want it. As I
want it. Without ever stopping to ask
what you think. That makes me a
rebellious child, Lord. Help me
to remember to ask your
opinion of what I'm about to do...
or think I should do. Help me
to seek your will.

Maker and Keeper

You are the maker and keeper of it
all, Lord, You are our maker and keeper.
Solid, powerful and everlasting.
Full of glory. Full of love. God,
have mercy on us, sinners.
Forgive us as you have promised.
Draw us to yourself, Lord, Keep
on drawing us even when
we resist. Don't give up on us.

Your Presence

Worthy art thou, Oh Lord, of my
interest, my time, my attention, my
thoughts, my admiration, my respect,
my love, my devotion, my awe
and my praise. But how often,
Lord, I confess that I give all
these to less worthy than
you. Help me learn daily to
bow before you, filled
and complete with your presence.

Great Love

Lord, you have made everything so
simple and so clear. And I, again and
again, seem to make it more
complicated. Help me to grasp
the simplicity as well as the vastness
of your great power, your
great majesty, your great
wisdom, your great glory
and most of all
your great love for me.

Loving Call

Lord, I know you have always
loved me, cared for me, watched
over me, called me again and again
to come to you. And how long and
how many times I have said you
surely don't want me because
I am so sinful.
Today help me to hear again your
loving call and to answer: OK,
Lord, here I am. You already
know me. And still you want me.
So just as I am I run to you and
say, Lord, I love you.

Lead Me

You lead me when I let you, Lord. But oh how I resist being lead. I want to be strong. I want to be in control. I want to call the shots. I want to figure things out. Help me to relax...to stop trying to do your job...to see you as you are and me for what I am. To trust you without reservation or fear.

Stop Running

I need you every hour. I run and run and run until I remember again—and am amazed each time I stop to consider it—that you have always loved me. You have never stopped loving me. Help me to stop running. To remember your love. And to respond by rising from my failings, by turning from deceptive voices and by coming to be surrounded and protected by your might. And sealed with the mark of your Spirit: a pure love for you.

Not Cleaned Up

Lord, most of all today I'm thankful that you accept us while we are not cleaned up; while we are still weighed down with sin, while we are still not sure who we are, what we believe and while we are not real sure who you are and what you are up to.
We are amazed that you like us. And, having experienced and enjoyed your acceptance, we are amazed at ourselves sometimes for how easy it is to condemn each other. How natural it seems. How good it makes us feel. Forgive that great flaw in us, Lord. Give me, and each of us, the grace to accept...not condemn. To be givers of life...not life sentences. To be providers of hope...not shame.
For you, lord, have accepted us, given us
life and provided hope.

Practice Forgiveness

Lord, most of all today I'm thankful that you figured out forgiveness and didn't leave it up to us to figure out. I'm ashamed, Lord, of how lightly we take your forgiveness and how tightly we hold on to our grudges and hurt feelings; and our perverse delight in remembering wrongs done to us, whether real or imagined. We have practiced keeping score instead of practicing forgiveness. We want you to forgive us, but we have such a hard time forgiving each other. Grant me, and each of us, Lord, the grace to practice forgiveness.
Today. And every day.

Light of Truth

Lord, most of all today I'm thankful that you keep our hearts tender enough to see our sins, at least occasionally. Because if it were left up to us, Lord, we would, for the most part, go on deluding ourselves about our goodness. We would, so often, choose to deal with our internal tensions, as best we can, rather than to confess our sins. Grant me, and each of us, Lord, the grace to see ourselves in the light of truth. Deliver us from the daily temptation of spiritual make-believe. We believe you love us, Oh God. Help our unbelief.

Faithful

Lord, most of all today I'm thankful that you are not capricious but steady; not fickle but faithful; not erratic but dependable; not devious but trustworthy. We count on your always being there and always being the same. Lord, sometimes we have a hard time trusting you. It's not you, Lord. It's us. You have shown us what you are up to and what you are made of, and we believe it. Help our unbelief. And grant me and each of us the grace to trust you every day. In the good times In the very good times. In the bad times and in the very bad times. *For your steadfast love never ceases. Your mercies never come to an end. They are new every morning. Great is your faithfulness. You are our portion. Therefore we will hope in you.*

Abundance

Lord, most of all today I'm thankful for the lives of the men and women in this room. You have blessed us beyond our ability to comprehend. You have shielded us from much that many in the world must endure. You have allowed us to have such an extravagant abundance of things. We enjoy peace and prosperity, and we see that so much of the world has neither. Why us, Lord? What do you have in mind for us? Have you spared us and blessed us for a reason? Is there something you want us to be or do because of where we are, what we have? Grant me, and each of us, the grace to search our hearts for your will, to listen for your voice and to follow your call whenever and wherever we hear you.

Hard Cases

Lord, most of all today I'm thankful that you are so much better than we are. From your perspective, we can only imagine how easy it would be to look at us and see losers, outsiders and impossible hard cases. How thankful we are, Lord, eternally thankful, that you see us with eyes of love and acceptance. Grant me, and each of us, the grace to see each other and all your children through eyes of love, compassion and acceptance.

OCCASIONS

Just Enough

In all our kingdom activities, even right now as we ordain and
bless these men and women, we don't know what else to do
but seek to know you and discover your will. Who are you?
What do you want? We wait. Listen. Discuss. Analyze. Ask you
again and again. Sometimes we hear clearly. Other times not
so much. What we hope for is just enough. Not to know, but
to believe enough to trust you. Enough to move forward.
Enough to make commitments.
Then, as without options, we turn again to you
and say: we've done our best. To know you.
To honor your will. Now, Lord, you must take
over our efforts and make of them what you will.
Whatever you will.
Oh, yes, Lord. Whatever you will...on earth
as it is in heaven.

And so we bring you now all our considerations of what it
means now and tomorrow to ordain: to invest officially
the authority over the church. Authority, yes, but moreover
the spiritual care and keeping of the church. Each of us.
And so what can we do but gently, gently lift these elder-men,
these shepherd-men and their wives, into your presence—
into your care—for your blessing.
Not with timidity but with boldness and confidence
that you will carry on the work of prayer and
discernment which we have begun. To accomplish your
purposes among us in this church as we grow into a
presence of service in your community.

What do we ask on behalf of these men and women, Lord? We ask
first that you capture the heart and imagination of each one and fill
each with your spirit and a love for your church. Protect each one
from the enemy who falsely accuses. Visit each one daily and

provide just what each one needs—those things that only you know and only you can provide.
In their hours of success and accomplishment, be, oh Lord, the one they credit and praise. In their dark hours of frustration and disappointment, please, Lord, be their refuge, their hope,

their strength and their salvation. Their way of escape.
Bind their hearts with the unity of love and peace. Bind them to us, us to each other, and all of us to you. Otherwise we don't know what to say, how to live or what to hope for. Amen.

OCTOBER 3, 2010
UPON THE ORDINATION OF NEW ELDERS
HIGHLAND OAKS CHURCH DALLAS

Change Agents

Blessed art thou, O Lord our God, King of the Universe,
who creates and brings every good blessing to us.
Hear O Israel, the Lord our God, the Lord is one.
Thou shalt love the Lord thy God with all thy heart.
Above all, O Lord, you have been faithful and
steadfast and we are still inclined to go our
own way. To want things our way. To
insist on our own way. Even to fight for
our own way. To the detriment of relationships
and the church, and to the potential imperilment
of our souls. Lord Jesus Christ, Son of God,
have mercy on us, sinners.

We claim that mercy now, Lord. And thank you
for your faithfulness to encourage us in times
of trouble. To comfort us with compassion in
our times of loss and confusion. To walk with us
and lead us through times of great change,
trial and challenge. In our personal lives,
our marriages and families, our communities
and especially our churches.
And we feel our need for you now maybe more
than ever before, Lord, as we move into arenas of
ever-increasing unfamiliarity, uncertainty and challenge.
I ask now your special blessing on this assembly of

your servants who provide the guidance and wisdom
of administering the kingdom's business in and
through our churches.
Deliver them from self-assuredness and lead them
into running to you with the full assurance that
you know, you see, you care, and that it is
you, always and only you, who is in charge of

each situation, large or small. And that your wisdom
is always available. And always best.
O Lord, as our culture changes, and our churches
change, deliver them and us also from a spirit of
timidity or resentment or resistance. Help each to

become a change agent led by your hand. To accomplish
what you want. To become what you want us to be.
To re-focus on what you think is important. To invest
in what you value. To stop what you don't value. And to
start what you tell us is worthy. O Lord, please, please
deliver us from having to have our own way as we
walk boldly and securely in your embrace into times
and arenas of service, ways of speaking and being and
doing which we can yet only imagine, and which we
dare not venture without your constant care.
Make us each into servants of your design, Lord, then
lead us each step of the way as we learn again to walk by faith.

INVOCATION
2010 CHURCH ADMINISTRATOR NETWORK FORUM

For Andrea and Alan

O Lord, our God, you are love.
Our minds can barely grasp the
depth and richness of this truth.
But we know. For
in all we see—there you are,
in all we feel—there you are,
in all we experience—there you are.
In each breath of each hour, in
every touch, every desire,
every fulfillment, every dream,
every accomplishment and
every challenge—there you are
shedding your love into our hearts and lives.

Now we ask the favor of your blessing
on Andrea and Alan as they become one
united soul—two in one. Give them
a special measure of this love. Enrich
their life together with your love. Teach
them gently to love each other. And to
diffuse your love to every person and
each situation they encounter. Help them
daily to let your love be the rule of
their life together. So that all may
see and know that you alone are
Lord. You alone are worthy of our
allegiance. You alone are love.

MARCH 2010
WEDDING RECEPTION INVOCATION

Three in One

Blessed art thou, O Lord our God, King of the Universe.
You are holy beyond our capacity to understand, but we know
we are not holy. You are good above anything to which
we might aspire, and we are sinners.
And so it is with reverence and awe that we come as
a group into your presence and ask you to join this assembly
as the object of
our confession,
our adoration,
our worship,
our praise
and our requests.
We ask this hour for a fresh start.
For clean hearts.
For a complete make-over.
A new birth.
Because, Lord, we don't know how to clean ourselves up,
to undo our pasts or to escape the bondage we have created for
ourselves. It seems, in fact, o Lord our God, that there is no hope,
no avenue, no way to improve our standing in your sight
except by your divine intervention. So calm us down, Lord,
and help us be still before you. Give us, one more time,
that fresh breath of your Holy Spirit.
Pour out on us the unpredictable, the mysterious, the divine.
Bring us your wind of cleansing.
We welcome your heavenly action, and we will
praise, praise the Father,
praise the Son,
and praise the Spirit, Three in One.
O praise him, o praise him!
Alleluia! Alleluia! Allelluia!
Amen. Amen. And all the church said Amen.

Highland Oaks Church Invocation
July 2009

We Need You Now

O Lord, our God, we need you now more than we ever have. Please give us each and as a team keen spiritual vision to see what you want for us...for our church. Soften our hearts so we can hear you. Slow us down so we can keep pace with the Spirit. Steel our wills against anything selfish. Bind us up in your love and wisdom so we can know the way to go. And please, Lord, please keep us on track as we seek your will.

And for those who will come to us for visits we ask your blessing. Please, Lord, take care of each one. Give each an extra measure of spiritual discernment in his decision making. Cleanse the heart of each to the degree that we may see you in each other. Raise up whomever you please, Lord, to come be a servant among us. Prepare and purify that heart right now for the days to come.

And for our church, Lord, we beg you, please revive us again. Help us as a body to love you more. And help us to love each other. And help us then to love the world...our neighbors...whom you love and who need you so much. Turn us around, Lord, to look toward you for all we are, all we want, all we need. Steadfastly overrule us when we

move and act and speak as if you were not our great, wise and loving God. Forgive us now, Lord, as we confess our great need for you today and tomorrow and all our tomorrows.

HIGHLAND OAKS CHURCH 2009
BEFORE CALLING A NEW PASTOR

Don't Let Go

Lord, this room is full of your men and women who make our churches work. They process each item of business that keeps us in business. Each system, department, ministry and program requires their careful scrutiny, comprehensive evaluation and wise counsel. We have entrusted to them the keys to your kingdom on earth. And, quite frankly, Lord, we expect them to be proficient experts in every arena—to mete out wisdom and justice in all matters. And to always take our call and make time for whatever new challenge we think up.

For this they need more strength, courage and resilience than any is capable of without your help. So now, Lord, I ask you to see this assembly of servants as a strong academy which depends on you for empowerment. They have answered the church's call for service, and now we join them in calling out to you to provide what only you can provide. Give them each, Lord, your full measure of strength, resolve and tenacity. Of wisdom, judgment and insight. And of gentleness, temperance and love.

I ask especially, Lord, that you would gift each of these leaders with an inspired vision of what our churches may become. Vision to see beyond our perennial efforts of self-sustainment to an era when we are salt to a disintegrating culture, light to a darkening society and leaven to a hungry world. To a time when all the ways we do church and all the ways we live our lives become a brilliant reflection of your goodness, your majesty, your caring heart, your acceptance, your forgiveness, your strength, your tenderness and your love.

And along that journey of vision and getting the job done, I ask also, Lord, that you become now and always, every day and every night, the helper and defender for each of these church heroes. Claim their hearts for yourself. Don't let go of them. Don't turn them loose. Bind yourself to each of them in very real ways so they may never doubt for a minute that you are on their side. That the work they do is your work. That the cause they champion is your cause. That the church they lead and serve is a vital and imperishable part of your kingdom on earth.

Protect them from the evil one, Lord. Be a shield before them as they move us step by step to become what you want us to be. Lead them not into temptation, Lord. And deliver them from anything— everything—that would take their eyes off of you. Comfort them when they are hurt or discouraged. Strengthen them when they are weary from the work. Guide their feet onto paths of righteousness. Remove obstacles that would slow them down. Embrace them with the great, holy affection we all need—which comes only from you.

And now as our savior Jesus has taught us, we are bold to say:
Our Father, who art in heaven, hallowed by thy Name,
thy kingdom come,
thy will be done, on earth as it is in heaven.
Give us this day our daily bread.
And forgive us our trespasses, as we forgive those who trespass against us.

And lead us not into temptation, but deliver us from evil.
For thine is the kingdom, and the power, and the glory, forever and ever.
Amen.

INVOCATION
2009 CHURCH ADMINISTRATOR NETWORK FORUM

Blessed Art Thou

Blessed Art Thou, our God, King of the Universe.
O Lord our God, who makes all things new,
speak to us as a whole people today. May your truth touch
not just our intellects, but also our deeper yearnings of
heart and soul. We bring with us now our daily concerns, as
well as our more eternal questions. May your
new creation in us shed light upon our everyday walk.

O God, we trust in your power to create, sustain, to enable. But
we could not trust if we did not know you are always
near. Be with us, Lord, as we are gathered here to worship you.
Help us not to check our minds or our hearts at the door,
but enable us to bring all that we are to you,
so that we might experience your touch upon
all aspects of our life.

Almighty God, unto whom all hearts are open, all desires
known, and from whom no secrets are hidden: cleanse
the thoughts of our hearts by the inspiration of your
Holy Spirit, that we may perfectly love you, and worthily
magnify your holy name in this assembly.

O God, who has made of one blood all the people of the earth,
and did send your blessed Son to preach peace to
those who are far off and to those who are near: grant that
people everywhere may seek after you and find
you, bring the nations into your fold, pour out your Spirit
upon all flesh, and hasten the coming of thy
kingdom; through thy Son Jesus Christ, our Lord,
who lives and reigns with
thee and the Spirit, one God, now and forever.

Highland Oaks Church Invocation
March 2009

Lucas Waits

Someone has posted an eviction notice! As if
I might delay on purpose the day I get
to join the party. This place has always been
temporary. A kind of purgatory between
what I can't tell you about because you
would never believe it and what you call
fresh air. And a little room to move around,
thank you very much.

Evicted! As if by choice I'd stay here
instead of out there with you! Listen,
you think you've got me figured out—
named and all. But let me
tell you, I will bring sunlight into your
world like nothing you've ever imagined. And
I will teach you things you thought beyond
your grasp.

Because I've spent time in a place
that doesn't need the sun for light. And
there I learned how things
really are. And how
God dreams.

ANTICIPATING BIRTH OF LUCAS GRAVES 2009

Ring Into Our Future

Blessed art thou, O Lord our God, King of the universe. We cannot approach an occasion of celebration like this without going back in time to remember your generous and constant outpouring of blessings on this church for so long a time. From our earliest days, when this city was young, to this very hour, you, O Lord, have been faithful. You have spoken into our lives with challenge, commission and comfort. With correction, counsel and consolation. When we've been down you have lifted us up. When we have stood too tall for our own good you have brought us down. In all and through all you have blessed us as a kind, thoughtful and wise provider.

Now we ask, O Lord our God, that you would ring into our future. Be to us and all who follow, for all the generations you have in mind to be your people in this place, our savior, our redeemer, our guide, our provider, our rock and our salvation. Above all else, O Lord, have mercy on us and forgive our sins. And teach us to forgive each other and ourselves. We seek your heart, O Lord. We want to walk in your way. We want to do your will—your way. We want to know you and love you first, best and always. And we want to learn to love our neighbor. Please, Lord, help us learn anew how to let your light of love shine in the world.

Today, Lord, we dedicate our new bell tower. We dedicate it to you. And we say, here, Lord, we mark the spot where our lives have been intersected by your love and your life. Again and again and again. Grant, Lord, that each note of each chime will remind us today and all our tomorrows that we are yours. We belong to you. May each note inspire us to love you more, to remember and renew our vows of loyalty to you, and to lift up our hearts—our lives—to you. And most of all, Lord, may our hearing of the chimes move

us to ring out your love and grace to our community
—the Good News
of Jesus, the call to discipleship, the sweet tones of salvation, care
concern, help, affection and acceptance for all people.

Bell Tower Dedication, Highland Oaks Church
March 2009

Breath of God

O Lord, our God, no one can name the hour
or place the breath of your Spirit will
stir and your presence appear,
creating from nothing new beginnings—
each occurrence a miracle and proclamation
that you are the one true God of all time
for all people.

Your presence inhabits the history of our
church—from most courageous and
humble beginnings to this present day
with lifetimes of sincere pioneers
seeking your will, depending on
your faithfulness, rejoicing in
your deliverance, your salvation—

and your abiding presence gives us
the necessary inspiration and
strength to stay the course of
our heritage. We lean today not on
our history or the legacy of our
founders, but as ever did they,
on you, O Rock of Ages.

Breathe upon us again, O Lord, and
create us anew as you would have
us be in this place and time.
Move among us and be our
strength as we reflect your great heart
of love to our community, setting
aside all but the radiance of grace.

Equip us for continued outrageous acts of
service, of good works, of

charity, of right living. Wash us once more
in the healing, cleansing stream of
your goodness as we continue to build
a sanctuary of generosity, hospitality,
mercy and encouragement.

Teach us ever to withhold judgment
and always to offer the comfort
of friendship with you. Instruct us
to be humble before you and aware
always that every moment of every
day we spend with you is a
sacred and precious gift.

Lead us with your tender hand into
the days of our future, O Lord. Sharpen our
faith as we learn to share your life with
an ever-changing culture. Be our spiritual
home as we look forward with your
blessing to years more of kingdom service while
ever, always looking back to the cross of Jesus.

DEDICATION OF TEXAS HISTORICAL MARKER
CELEBRATING HIGHLAND OAKS CHURCH
150TH ANNIVERSARY IN 2005
AUGUST 2008

Revive Them Again

Lord, behold these your servants.
The ones we depend on to get things done.
The ones who work so much behind the scenes.
The ones who are usually unheralded,
sometimes unappreciated,
too often unthanked
and nearly always expected to accomplish the impossible
in an unreasonably short time
with little or no notice;
to orchestrate without flaw the
programs of the church in such an expert
manner as to please everyone—
every time—
leaving fully satisfied
the dreamers
the workers
the staff
the volunteers
all the members, hot and cold,
and the community at large.

We rely on them to balance the budget,
yet still somewhere find the funds for
expansion of operations,
repair and maintenance of aging facilities
and with a ready smile always to approve
every new idea, ministry, program,
upgrade and improvement.
All the while maintaining complete and total harmony
among
a divergent staff
a starry-eyed pastor
a stationary eldership

and a transient, sometimes fickle membership.

Look with kindness, understanding and compassion
on them, Lord.
For these blessings you may be their sole source.
Repair their frayed nerves with your peace.
Restore their vision with your light.
Renew their strength with your life.
Reduce their stress with your grace.
Relieve their anxiety with your comfort.
Return their joy with your mercy.
Remove temptation from their path with your guidance.
Rekindle their love of the kingdom with your blessing.
Revive them again with your Spirit.

And, Lord, when they are undone, be their healer.
When they are exhausted, be their strength.
When they are discouraged, be their friend.
When they are overwhelmed, be their comfort.

In the dark hours of doubt, be their truth.
In their frightening hours of fear, be their courage.
In the aftermath of discord, be their peace.

Provide safe paths for them to walk in, Lord.
Shelter them from all harm.
Lead them not into temptation.
Deliver them from evil.

Call them each hour to your side, Lord, to be
your servant, to first and last honor and serve
you, to run to you for help, to praise you freely
for success and to sense always
your presence
your creative touch
your caring gaze
your forgiving heart

in all they do for all the rest of us.
As together we
work
wait
hope
and pray
for your
will to be done on earth
as it is in heaven.

INVOCATION
2008 CHURCH ADMINISTRATOR NETWORK FORUM

Prayer for the Church

Oh Lord, our God, we marvel at your faithfulness.
We celebrate your care and attention.
We acknowledge everything belongs to you and
you have it all under control.

When we have lost our way, there you are.
When our strength is gone, there you are.
When we make a mess of things, there you are.
When we are out of ideas, there you are.

When we are
exhausted
discouraged
confused
uncertain
wounded
there you are.

You are our defender.
You are worthy.
You are holy and forgiving.
You are faithful.

Our strength comes from you.
Our hope is in you.
Our future is in your hands.
Our faith is in your goodness.

Oh Lord give us vision.
Open our eyes to see clearly
ourselves,
each other,
the world that you love and
that so needs you.

And let us see you.

Oh Lord give us strength
to be what you want us to be
and do what you want us to do.

Oh Lord give us courage
to speak up for you when we can
and to be quiet enough—
often enough—
to listen for and hear
your voice.

Oh Lord give us wisdom
to know and do your will,
to humble ourselves
first before you
and always before each other.

Oh Lord give us your healing for
our self-inflicted wounds
which result when we go our own way
instead of
closely
carefully
following you.

Oh Lord help us to
forgive each other as you
have forgiven us.

Oh Lord help to
deny ourselves as individuals
for the sake of the church
and the kingdom.

Oh Lord help us learn

from our mistakes and become
better friends
better leaders
better followers
better citizens of the kingdom.

Oh Lord lead us
not into temptation.
Deliver us from evil.
Lead us in paths of righteousness
and beside still waters of peace and security
in you.

Oh Lord defend us
from the evil one
and from ourselves.

And please continue, Oh Lord, our God, to
move among us.
Help us get out of the way and
follow your lead
as individuals
as leaders
as a church.

As you have been in our past, Oh Lord,
and as you are so evidently in our present,
please be in our future
as day by day
we learn
again and again
that you are our great God.
There is no other like you.
And we desperately need you.

INVOCATION HIGHLAND OAKS CHURCH

Reunion

One of your best has left us and flown to you, Lord. There is sorrow here and rejoicing there. Open our spiritual eyes to see the beauty in this relocation. Touch our hearts to know how much our pain of loss is felt in heaven by your great heart of compassion.

How can we thank you, Lord, for a man like Sammie Swim? As we try to imagine what life will be like without him, we remember all the best part of you that we have been blessed to see in him. Your heart of love became flesh and lived with us, reminding us always of the Incarnate Son who did the same.

So now receive him back again to yourself, Lord, with the gratitude of all of us who loved him and were loved by him. We sing today as an echo of the heavenly choirs who in your presence, as he is now, sing *Holy, Holy, Holy!* to you day and night. Tune our hearts, Lord, as we rehearse for that bright day when we join Sammie and sing to you.

That reunion, already begun, becomes for us reason enough to ask you for our share of faith to *see in death the gate of eternal life.* Increase our faith, Lord,

*so that in quiet confidence we may continue
our course on earth, until, by your call,
we are united with* Sammie,
and with all those we have loved who
have gone before.

EULOGY PRAYER FOR SAMMIE SWIM
JULY 2008

Rushing In

I was trained for action, Lord.
For getting it done—not waiting to
see what will happen next. I
feel most useful and productive
when I confront a problem and
analyze the data
calculate the cost
measure the risk
then move quickly to find a
solution. Quite frankly, I'm
astonished to learn so late that
you do your best work in me when I am
still
quiet
waiting.

Your hand has been on me and I
have felt your guiding presence
much of the time, Lord, even
while I've been rushing in and
fixing what needed fixing
doing what needed doing
making decisions that needed making.
But now I wonder if I have been
trusting myself too much and
not really knowing what trusting you
might look like. Thank you, Lord,
for keeping up with me through the
years. Now help me slow down
so you can take a good look at me
while I learn to listen to you.

Do I dare ask you to search me

inside and out, Lord? Staying ever on the
move has lulled me into thinking maybe
you saw me as only a blur. If I
stop running will you look me over
and decide I'm not made of the right
stuff to do you any good? If you
put me to the test how will I do? Will
you like me after all is said and done?
Will you find any raw material worth
going to work on? Can you re-shape
an old runner into a vessel worthy
of your effort? Worthy of your time?
Worthy of your love? I'm willing to yield,
Lord, if you are still willing to work.

Have it Your Way

Now we launch a new year, Lord, and
as we have ever found it, this
one hasn't yet given us many clues
as to what lies in store. The only
truth we know for sure is the same
one we discovered last year—we
won't know what is down the road until we
start walking. So walk with us, please,

because our yesterdays have done their dismantling
work and in truth we find ourselves
fearful of taking that first calendar step.
For some of our families have been fractured
by loss of mother, father, husband, wife, child or
friend. And some of our hearts have been
splintered by grief, greed, rage,
disappointment, fear or uncertainty.

Find us now, Lord, cautious, wary and
desperately in need of more courage than
we can conjure by ourselves. Find us
now, Lord, in hope of days of light and
nights of peace. Find us now, Lord, in
postures of anticipation of your company.
Find us now in attitudes of waiting.
Find us yielded. Find us still.

We wait for your comfort—the sense
of your presence—that tells us all
is well. We wait for your vision—the
sense of direction—that leads us through
times and events we are afraid of without
you. We wait for your permission—that
sense of forgiveness—to move on to new,

unexplored worlds of life, love and service.

And through it all, Lord—our hesitancy, our not knowing the way, our brokenness, our grief, our frustrations, our fear— we seek your will. Come now. Speak to us. Shout if you must till we hear your voice. Come now. Lead us. Pull us if you must till we follow you. Wherever you want us to go. This year, Lord, have it your way.

Nothing in My Hand

I wanted to bring you the best of last year, Lord.
Something beautiful.
Or holy or special.
Something that would make you smile
on me—make you proud of me.
I looked and searched for just the
right gift, but as you see
I've come to you again with
nothing in my hand.

I thought of collecting my tears for you, Lord,
tears for my sins.
I found plenty of sins
and a pool of tears I'd shed.
But I was caught short in my collecting
by the streams of mercy that
washed over me—taking my
tears with it, leaving me clean and with
nothing in my hand.

Maybe my energy or my zeal or
my hours of work in the
kingdom could be bundled and
wrapped into a suitable gift for
you, Lord. But my gathering
and wrapping only produced a
shabby offering—not fit for a
king and surely not valuable enough
to exchange for your forgiveness.

Everything I tried to make into a gift
for you, Lord, from the inventory of
my life, turned out to be light
as air—my goodness, my

good works, my understanding,
my care, my intentions—
all collapsed into nothing. And in
truth I found myself naked,
helpless and very much in need.

Walk with me through this
year, Lord. Show me what
is real and valuable.
Open my eyes to my need
and to your bounty
so that at year's end
I may have the privilege
of coming to you—rescued, and
with nothing in my hand.

Unto Us

How sweet to our ears are the sounds
that proclaim *unto us a child is born,
unto us a son is given.* Sweet indeed, Lord,
and the best within us resonates with
child-like joy at those strains we hear
only once a year. Because when
we hear them we know for sure all
is well and you love us.

It is a season when many of us do righteous
battle with those seasonal demons who
become bold upon sensing Christmas
is near. Bold enough to
accuse us and remind us of
losses, failures and heartaches.
Bold enough to dare try their
best to do their worst in us.

Help us, Lord, to enjoy the beauty of
the Christ Child. Strengthen us
to fight back with all our might
against anyone, anything, any thing that
tries to deny us the
pleasure of rejoicing in our great and
priceless gift: *for unto us a child
is born, unto us a son is given.*

Through Christmas we will cling to you,
Lord, and we will cherish with
our deepest emotions that which we
can only barely understand—
that by giving us Jesus you gave us
life. You gave us yourself. You
planned and gathered your best
and made of it a gift unto us.

Lord of Lords

We welcome you, Jesus, coming
to us as a helpless baby,
ordained before time began to
reign over all creation as
Lord of lords,
King of kings.

We honor you, Jesus, growing
up as one of us, experiencing
all we experience,
knowing the hurt of rejection,
showing compassion while
living as the sinless God-man.

We listen to you, Jesus, as
you expose the heart of goodness
and expound the solid reality
of right and wrong,
good and evil, in plain
truths we can live by.

We marvel at you, Jesus, for
events in your life that we
have names for but can scarcely
comprehend. You overrule nature
with miracles of mercy. You show
the full glory of heavenly splendor.

We follow you, Jesus, because we
believe what you say and do is
true and good. Your example as
helper of the helpless inspires us every
day to find ways to live outside
ourselves in service of others.

We hail you, King Jesus, as
Lord of heaven and earth,
maker and ruler of all things,
provider of salvation and of
hope to all who will bend a
knee and bow before your authority.

We worship you, Lord Jesus,
King over all. One with the
Father and the Spirit. Living
in us and with us as constant
protector, knowing guide,
loving Savior.

Call to Worship

Is that your face we see, Lord?
In the rain,
the rainbow,
the twilight,
the dawn,
the sunshine,
the darkness—
is that you, Lord,
calling us
to worship?

Is that your voice we hear, Lord?
In children's laughter,
frightening thunder,
singing birds,
ocean's waves,
great symphonies,
church bells—
is that you, Lord,
calling us
to worship?

Is that your breath we enjoy, Lord?
In loving hugs,
sweet reunions,
friendship,
pardon,
encouragement,
inspiration—
is that you, Lord,
calling us
to worship?
Is that your Spirit we feel, Lord?

Ray Hardin

In stricken conscience,
broken hearts,
loneliness,
contagious joy,
hours of peace,
days of hope—
is that you, Lord,
calling us
to worship?

Give us, please, Lord,
new hearts
so we can
see your face,
hear your voice,
enjoy your breath
and feel your Spirit;
so we can
respond to you
in all the ways
you make yourself
known to us,
certain that
each one
is a
call to worship.

BELL TOWER GROUNDBREAKING
HIGHLAND OAKS CHURCH

Breakfast

I ask your blessings on me now, Lord.
On this house.
On this hour.
On this friendship.
On this food.
Give me, I pray, your blessings
of this day.
Whatever they may be.
However they may arrive.
Whenever you are ready to give,
help me be ready to receive.

I ask your blessings this friend now, Lord.
On his person.
On his family.
On his past, future and present.
On his ministry.
Give him now, I pray, your blessings
of this day.
Whatever they may be.
However they may arrive.
Whenever you are ready to give,
help him be ready to receive.

And I thank you, Lord,
for your gentle hand
of giving,
for your faithful way
of forgiving,
for your mysterious way
of revealing,
for your dependable way
of calling
us back to you—
always back to you.

Your Glory

Lord, it's your servant Ray again, talking to you on
behalf of this large room full of your people
who love you. First of all, Lord, be merciful
to me a sinner. Be merciful to each of us because
we have broken your commandments.
We have each depended far too much on ourselves
and far too little on you.
Forgive us, Lord. Reclaim us as your own.
Renew in us a deep and simple trust in you as our
God, our provider, our protector, our redeemer,
our savior, our friend, our Lord. Lead us to purity
of heart, Lord. Strengthen our resolve to love
and serve you first and best and always. Bolster
our faith, Lord, that we may always
acknowledge you, in all our ways—all our days—as
our unchanging, eternal king of the universe and
Lord of our hearts. Be with us Lord. We cannot
live without you. We dare not try to take one
step alone. We cannot bear the loads of
life unaided. We need your strength to lean
ourselves upon. Lord, all we have
comes from you. every nickel of our wealth.
Every minute of our health. Every breath.
Every dream. Every joy.
Teach us how to have grateful hearts.
Teach us to give it all away for your sake and for
your glory.

INVOCATION
HIGHLAND OAKS CHURCH

Thanksgiving

The season begs us to remember, Lord,
to give thanks to you or to
someone, somewhere for
the bounty of blessings we enjoy.
Even the newspaper calls us to
live lives of gratitude as a way
to enjoy good mental health.
And I wonder, Lord, if we have
begun believing in gratitude
as little more than another
self-help formula for successful living
or an expression of good manners
we expect from our children.

Teach us how to be grateful beyond
the season, Lord.
Touch us in that most secret chamber of
our hearts where we decide
hour by hour
who it is who provides for us
all we have, all we are—
whether it is ourselves we
most appreciate for the ability
to earn, provide and accumulate
or someone else.
Open our eyes, Lord, to see you as the
faithful provider.

For you, oh Lord our God, remain
faithful through the ages. Through
our times of celebration and
our days of loss and grief
you walk with us each step

and your light helps us find
our way.
You, oh Lord, are our
Rock of Ages.
Great is your faithfulness.
You never change.
You are the one true
constant in our lives.

You provide everything freely
because making and giving
are your nature,
the center of who you are.
Help our expressions
of thanksgiving to you become
our hourly custom
our daily habit
our worship
our meditation
our ritual
our liturgy
our nature.

At Year End

We remember now, Lord,
our year gone by—
a year of loss
of separation
of disappointment.
A year of not being
our true selves,
but less.
A year of lost
opportunity
to show kindness
to offer love
to provide forgiveness
to bestow comfort.

We ask your forgiveness
now, Lord.

But we also remember now, Lord,
our year gone by—
a year of
celebration,
joy,
comfort,
encouragement
and hope.
A year of victories
large and small
where we heard
your voice
and saw your face
if only for a
brief moment.

We pour out our thanks
now, Lord.
We face now a new year, Lord.
We know not
what it will bring.
Whether clouds of doubt
or sunshine of clarity;
whether deep grief
or unimagined joy;
whether steep hills of challenge
or green valleys of rest.
Whether days of anxiety
or weeks of calm.

We ask you now, Lord,
to be in each day
each step
each thought
each action
each endeavor.
We ask you now, Lord,
for a glimpse of
your love
your care
your guidance
your providence
for a touch
a smile
a surprise
to remind us again
and again
and again
that you are
ever present with us.
And that you call us

to hear your voice
to follow after you
and to pour ourselves
out in service
to each other.

We give you, Lord,
our year past.
We give you, Lord,
our days ahead.
For we can do
no more
and
no less.

Ending Well

We are ending a course of study, Lord.
We ask your blessing on
this study
so we may,
with you,
say it ended well.

We are ending another hour together, Lord.
We ask your blessing on
this time spent with
each other and with you
so we may know
it ended well.

And, Lord, you know we
face endings of
life's experiences, good and bad.
We ask your blessing on us
so that with your help
they may end well.

Swiftly comes the ending
of all endings
for each of us, Lord.
Be with us, Lord.
Grant for each of us the ultimate
victory of ending well with you.

Redeem It All

Blessed art thou, O Lord our God, King of the universe. Our rock. Our redeemer. Our healing and our salvation. We put our hearts into submission to you, Lord. Not because that always feels good, but because when we don't, we suffer tough days and worse nights. And we usually, finally regret that we didn't take that submissive posture

from the beginning of things. So teach us, Lord, how to ask for, respect, accept and follow your guidance in all we do. As we manage the affairs of our churches, please, Lord, please let us lean on you, learn from you, depend on you in all things. In all times. Even occasions gone by. We remember some of them with regret and some with joy

and gratification. As we look back on where we've been, help us to forgive ourselves and others for opportunities missed. For things not done well. Deliver us from our recurring need to re-write the past, confident that you, Lord, can and will redeem even our worst mistakes. Soften our hearts, Lord, to see that redeeming. And as we walk

and work, we ask for courage to face the challenges of each day. To live in the present, not avoiding the demands of what must be done now. Deliver us from carrying the heavy load of pre-conceived ideas and solutions which may have been effective yesterday. Give us fresh insights of Kingdom health today—each day. And bless our

efforts to redeem each day's work for your glory. But moreover, Lord, strengthen us for what lies ahead. For the tomorrows of our work, our church, our people, programs and plans. Please, Lord, give us vision for what may be. Deepen our hope that you will instruct us and guide us even on paths we cannot yet

see. Or sometimes even imagine. Light a spark of holy
imagination for the future. Grant us abiding confidence that
you will walk with us, work through us and ultimately
accomplish your will among us in scenes not yet
revealed. We trust you also to redeem our future and
the life of the church as we grow, change and move closer

to you. All the while, and above all, Lord, as we manage
money, debt and budget, membership and involvement, facilities
and stewardship, education and outreach, justice and
mercy, inspiration and comfort, discipling and discipline, teach us,
please, Lord, to hear what it really is we are to do and be.
Help us to see the big picture of our work—and yours.

Join us, Lord, in remembering and redeeming our past;
in committing to face present challenges and needs;
in pledging to take your hand
as we live into
our future
with you.

INVOCATION FOR CHURCH ADMINISTRATOR'S
NETWORK FORUM

2011

Crying Out

I Am the Blind Man

Lord, without you I am the blind man.
Sitting on the sidelines of life, I am
a beggar. Hoping someone will notice
me and toss me some
spare change. Maybe enough to make
it for one more day. My hope of
anything better has long since vanished.
And I am reduced to despair.

Lord, without you I am the blind man.
I can't see the beauty of the world.
A smile escapes my notice. A sunset
fades unseen. A friend's need goes
unmet in my darkness. And your
bounty and beauty are wasted
on me because no light gets
into my eyes or brightens my way.

Lord, without you I am the blind man.
How did all this start? Did
my vision begin to fail when my
pride began to rule? Did my sight
dim when carelessness or
greed gained a foothold in my heart?
Have I for so long depended on
myself instead of you that darkness won the day?

Lord, without you I am the blind man.
Pass by, please, one more time
and call me to your side. I'll tell
you, as before, that what I want—
what I need—more than anything
else is to see clearly. I want to see
your face. I want to see what is real.
I want to see you and follow, praising.

The Search

Our search for answers has been genuine, Lord.
We really have wanted to learn how
to live good lives. How to find
comfort in our own skins.
How to be mature and responsible.
Something deep inside us resonates still
with the challenge to
be all we can be.
Our vocabulary from bedroom to boardroom
has been punctuated with
symbols of success and achievement.
Yet we are left with our questions unanswered
and our dreams gone blank.
Did our search lead us in
the wrong directions, Lord?
What might we have learned from you?

Our search for wisdom has been relentless, Lord.
We really have tried to discover the
secret behind contentment and joy.
Our shelves are lined with countless
volumes that outline simple
formulas for growing up.
We have tried them all
yet still find ourselves
back at the starting gate as
uninformed as ever—still
longing for something just beyond
our reach.
Has our search taken us off
the real path of maturity?
What might we have learned from you?

Rescue us, please Lord, from our
exhausting pursuit of all the good
things we need to know
and long to live.
Help us turn around and find
in you the answer to all our questions
the solution for all our riddles
the satisfaction of all our needs.
Help us learn from you.

What Is It?

What is it you want me to be, Lord? Are there
attitudes in me that make you unhappy? Or
dispositions I take for granted in
myself that you would, for my good, amend?
And if so, Lord, though it be late in the game,
please keep re-making me—
re-shaping me—
into the sort of person you want me to be.

What is it you want me to hear, Lord? Have
you been trying to speak to me while I have not
been listening? Is there a message
you've been wanting me to hear that I've
been tuning out? If so, purify my hearing,
Lord, so I can learn to receive your
communications—in whatever form you may
choose to send them my way.

What is it you want me to know, Lord? Do you
have lessons waiting for me to learn? Perhaps
great truths I've not yet grasped about you,
about me or about everyone
around me? Be my teacher, Lord, now
and ever. Discipline me to be your
eager student—ready ever to absorb all
you would have me learn.

What is it you want me to do, Lord? Are there
important jobs you've saved for me? Or—
more likely—little things I've been
overlooking? Challenges to take
on? Habits to leave off? Words you

want me to say? Silence you wish me
to keep? Give me courage, Lord, to be and
hear, know and do what you, not I, want.

Looking Good

Oh Lord God, we are so happy to know that
you see beauty in our hearts whether or not
we wear physical beauty as bodies.
It isn't, Lord, that we disdain beauty—most
of us are heavily invested in looking good, or
at least as good as we can. We
thank you for beauty of all kinds and
consider it a wonderful gift from you.

But deliver us, please, Lord, from any
inordinate desire to achieve or maintain
good looking flesh at the expense of
neglecting the spiritual grooming you
appreciate most. Work there with us,
Lord, to craft everlasting beauty. Help us
grow up as we grow older...to keep doing
what we can with our outsides and our insides.

If you purposely designed us to age
and fade so that our beauty
may ultimately be replaced by
yours—shining from the inside out—
we ask you, Lord, for moments of clear
vision ever so often...just enough
to keep us on track with the progress
you are making in us.

It's the Waiting

O Lord we are beginning to believe that maybe
you do have plans for us—something
special in mind that
only you could come up with,
only you could make happen,
only you could see through
to completion. What joy it brings us to
think you are that interested in us.

For a long time, Lord, we've figured that your best design
for us would kick in after we have died—
immortality
heaven
singing angels
flung crowns.
And maybe a new body but to tell you the truth
we've never been real sure about that.

But is it something in the here and now that you
have figured out for us?
Something you want us to do?
Something you want us to be?
Are there big accomplishments of grace or little triumphs of
generosity you are waiting for us to get started on?
Neighbors to love?
Enemies to forgive?

Of course there is all that instruction in
the Bible about how we are to live. All
the talk about putting you first and
loving others and not being worldly
and silly but spiritual and grown up.
But frankly, Lord, we've already pretty much
concluded we can't do that, unless...could it be

those things are part of your plan?

Most of us muddle through, Lord, doing
the best we can on good days and forgetting
to pay attention much of the time. Maybe
we have diluted the whole thing to a wish
and occasional prayer that you will
some day, somehow speak to us and
let us know what you have in mind.
But honestly, Lord, the hard part is the waiting.

Heart Surgery

Create in me a clean, heart, O Lord my God, because I'm pretty sure that much, maybe most, of the unhappiness and conflict I encounter is due to my having gotten dirty and messed up the one you gave me. Nothing intentional, Lord. I didn't set out to soil or foul your gift. In fact, I've made pretty good—diligent even—effort to cultivate your life within mine. But

something has gone wrong. I'm not reacting right. My patience has melted into hair trigger readiness to blame and accuse. I am harboring—just barely concealing—hot judgment against some who don't see things as I do. And as I assume they should see them, too. Which, I've got to tell you, Lord, is a real conversation-stopper. And a huge affection-killer. And I am left in a seriously lame

position here with my brothers and sisters in your church—sometimes thinking about running away instead of what appears to be what I really need: heart surgery. So have at me, Lord, when you are ready. Open me up. Do the mending only you can do. Then give me, please, an extra measure of faith to recuperate and heal in your loving care, O Great Physician.

Don't Forsake Us

We are walking around in a fog, Lord, undone by
our own clumsy attempts to have our way
and be in charge of how things will turn out.
We have sacrificed your gifts of
love
joy
peace
on the questionable altar of
putting ourselves first
others second and
you last.
For a season we have forgotten that
you are in charge of everything.
We have denied that if we are to experience
any rest
any restoration
any inward stillness
we must first loosen our grip
on outcomes
circumstances
each other
and trust you to take care of us.

Come into the mess we have made, Lord.
We are embarrassed to invite you in
but we simply have no choice.
Please come in and bring us a fresh supply
of all you offer
which we desperately need.
Bring us
hearts broken for the right reasons and
healing for our broken hearts.
Bring us

clear vision of how soiled we are and
the cleansing we are afraid of but
cannot live without.
Bring us
sorrow for the hurt we have caused and
mending for our hurting sorrow.
Bring us
forgiveness which we seem somehow

to have misplaced.
Bring us
hope for days of service and
nights of rest.
Bring us
enough humility for each of us
to have enough
and some to spare.
Bring us
the light of your presence
to drive out the uncertainty and fear
that moved in and tried to
run our house.

Come to our rescue, please, Lord.
Don't give up on us.
Please don't give up on us.
And above all, Lord, please
don't forsake us.

Peace on Earth

Did something go wrong, Lord?
Was there a flaw in the plan?
Did you change your mind?
Are we somehow part of the problem?
What was it we misunderstood
when you told us that Jesus
was to be your Prince of Peace?

All we see in the world is conflict
and tension. Nations too ready
to declare war and so reluctant
even to discuss a plan for peace.
Old familiar hostilities eclipsed
by new feuds between rising
powers all too ready to rattle sabers.

Our own nation pulses with
unrest and simmers with
thinly-veiled hostility between
right and left, bears and bulls,
federalists and states' right advocates.
Post modern pluralists seethe with
disdain at conservatives who volley in kind.

Racial tensions and perennial
divisions between rich and poor,
gay and straight and liberal and
conservative rock our city. We
argue about immigration and
tollways infringing on long-dreamed-of
aquatic parks while the homeless stay hungry.

Our church provides some refuge from
all the confusion and posturing.

But even here we sense potential discord
bubbling just beneath the surface.
Shall we forge ahead or cherish tradition?
Who is in charge? What are we about?
Will we find our way and be a light?

Even our families are fragmented, Lord.
Some believe. Some snub your message.
Moms and dads too often look like
frantic business partners rather than
lovers, friends and parents.
Our children often seem adrift on a
stormy sea of isolation and desperation.

And deep within ourselves, Lord,
we sometimes feel confused, harried,
hurried and unsure where we belong
or what direction we should turn next.
Sometimes our best efforts are not
nearly sufficient to keep us
anchored in wisdom, good judgment or you.

Rescue us, Lord, from ourselves.
Heal our world with your passionate love.
Call our country back to you—you alone.
Calm our city with reasonable stability.
Refine our church with your fire of grace.
Infuse our families with mighty healing life.
Enter our hearts, Lord, and give us peace on earth.

We Didn't Listen

Your warnings were plain enough, Lord.
We just didn't listen.
From the very beginning you
told us to stay away from
forbidden fruit, but
we found it so alluring—
and sweet—surely one bite
wouldn't hurt anything.
But one taste was never
enough for us, Lord.
One taste only made us
want more.
You told us to
leave it alone—
for our own good—
but we didn't listen.

You made it perfectly clear, Lord,
that we should not take things
that don't belong to us.
You tediously explained
that we shouldn't even
look longingly at others' treasures
and wish they were ours.
You warned us that
once we started
wanting for ourselves
what others had
we'd soon be helpless
to stop.
Oh, you made it
simple enough, Lord,

but we didn't listen.

When you described the altars
that lesser gods would demand
us to sacrifice upon, Lord,
we rolled our eyes and sighed aloud
thinking you didn't
appreciate just how
good and strong we are.
Only we were wrong.
And you were right.
Our pursuits have led us
away from you and
toward the siren song
of plenty which
sounded so good but offered
only empty promises.
Oh, you told us, Lord.
But we didn't listen.

As if in a daze
we found ourselves
worshipping at the altars of
wealth
fame
knowledge
correctness
power
authority
and goodness.
We thought you
wouldn't notice, Lord.
Or that you wouldn't care.
We had to learn the
hard way what you told us
all along. We didn't listen.

And now we stand before you, Lord,
ragged
broke
worn out
and finally disillusioned
with the lies
we've been told—
and we've believed.
We bring you our
broken hearts
wasted years
bad habits and
greedy spirits.
And as only beggars can,
we beg forgiveness.
We thought we could have it all.
And we just didn't listen.

Starting Over

When things go really well, Lord,
and I'm on top
of my game—
when I get what I want
and I feel good about
myself;
when my plans work out
and I'm at peace with the
world;
when things get done
and the way seems
clear—
then, Lord, it's pretty easy
for me
to give you thanks
and even some credit.

But when things fall apart, Lord,
and I'm down and out,
under a heavy load—
when what I want seems
out of reach;
when nothing I begin
gets finished;
when I'm discouraged,
frustrated or dismayed
and I don't know where
to turn—
then, Lord, its really hard
for me
to give you thanks

and even some credit.

In fact, Lord, you are
the first one
I'm likely
to blame
in those bad times.
Why are you holding out
on me?

Why won't you come to
my rescue?
Why can't you give me
a break?
And
why won't you live up to
your reputation
of steadfast love
and great compassion?

But even as I say these words, Lord,
I sense I'm making
a big mistake.
Maybe its not you
after all.
Maybe its
me.
Maybe I broke the chain
of fellowship
with you.
Maybe I hid my face
from you
too long.
Maybe I didn't include

you in
my plans.
Maybe I didn't want you
to really see me
when I was winning
or
when I was losing.

Can I start over again, Lord?
Can I begin by saying
how much I need you?...
and end by pleading,
have mercy on me,
O God.

To Tell You the Truth

There are times, Lord, when things don't go so well for us.
Times when we wonder just how long we can keep
up appearances and act like everything is alright.
Times when we ache deep inside that
most tender part of ourselves.
Times when we wonder if we can go on.
Times when we can almost taste the
bitterness within us that wants out.
Times when we wonder
why we are here.
And to tell you the truth, Lord,
times when we wonder
why you won't help us.

Please love us when we feel this way, Lord.
When we can't figure a way out,
be our escape.
When we can't come up with a solution,
be our salvation.
When we can't find an answer,
be our teacher.
When we can't overcome our fear,
be our courage.
When we can't banish our discouragement,
be our comfort.
When we simply don't know which way to turn,
be our guide.

Help us get over being embarrassed
around you, Lord.
We feel so guilty about letting things
get us down so much.
We know we are supposed to

Ray Hardin

trust you in all things.
And we want to, Lord.
We want to.
So start with our hearts and go to work
on us, Lord.
Make us over again in your image.
Because to tell you the truth, we are out
of ideas unless you come to our rescue.

Our Words

O Lord, our listener,
we have been far more interested
in our right to speak—
our freedom of speech—
than we have cared for
what you want to hear.

We speak sometimes, Lord,
in ways that show
we must think
you have lost
your hearing,
or that you
don't really care
what we say.

Our culture bombards us with
half-truths,
exaggerations,
empty promises
and too many words.
Bring us back to you, Lord.
Teach us again
how you want us
to speak.

Deliver us from talking too much.
Defend us from lying.
Soften our words.
Rescue us from sweet-tasting gossip.
Slow us down.
Keep slander from our lips.
And purify our hearts, Lord,
so that our words
may give life.

Dare We?

You, O Lord our God, have the answer to our
every question. You know and reveal all truth.
Dare we ask you? Could we handle the truth? How
should we feel if your explanations don't match our
expectations? What if your truth is vastly bigger
and more inclusive than we counted on? Dare we hear?

And you invite us to take long sips—gulps—of your
thirst-quenching water. With only the promise
that this Spirit-libation will become self-perpetuating.
Ending for all time in some mysterious
way our deepest longing to know, to feel, to become.
Dare we take the cup from your hand?

Soften our hearts, Lord. Give us a courage we've not
known before. Deepen our trust. Enliven our
confidence and faith in you as the changeless
provider who leads us into change; the loving
creator who keeps on re-making us in your image.
Tell us the truth, Lord. Give us a refreshing drink.

Cry Out

The people cry out in their oppression, O Lord, their lives and liberties hang now in delicate balance and memories of better days barely flicker in their imaginations. They cry out as families and friends are indiscriminately slaughtered. They huddle in fear inside their own houses—afraid to venture

out even for food or water. Not captives of foreign powers, the people are in bondage to their own leaders who have gathered in all profits and prosperity for themselves—sharing none or little with their own oppressed masses. The people

cry out, O Lord, in the same places and in the same way they ever have cried out. Won't someone help us? Can't someone deliver us from this too-familiar nightmare? You heard their cries in days of old. Please, Lord, hear their crying out again.

Ever We Ask

Ever we ask, Lord, why is there sin? Why is there suffering? Why must we endure loss, sorrow, disappointment and the accompanying pain of hurt that seems to have a life of its own? Not under our control. Not subject to our demands to leave us or even offer any explanation.

If you liked us better, Lord, couldn't you arrange some formula that would help us to at least understand? And if the offering from your hand must be short of that, then maybe a cook book with details of ingredients, preparation, timing and number of normal servings. Something to

ease the hours and years of numbness after we run up against some immovable obstacle we don't comprehend or know how to handle. Is it really sin that begets suffering? Or are you up to something we can't yet see? Open our eyes, Lord, to the light of your plan. Your glory. Ever we ask.

Thanks

True to Your Word

You made us, Lord, so you surely understand
our times of sorrow, fear, discouragement.
You know it is easy for us to honor and trust
you when everything is going well. And
it is often so hard for us to believe you are
still there when our bad times come.
Forgive our short memories and remind us
again that through our good times and
our bad times you have been
true to your word.

The strong promise of your enduring love
has never faded, Lord. From beginning
to end—and every minute in between—
our lives are rich beyond belief
because of how you love us. You have been
true to your word.

And for all our efforts to look our best
when we are at our worst, you have
consistently accepted us for who
we are, Lord. You alone demand no perfection
from our brokenness. You have been
true to your word.

When guilt is what we deserve and
what we feel, you always freely
forgive us, Lord. You alone require
no innocence from our fallen
lives. You have been
true to your word.

It is hard for us to fall on the sharp
edges of loss and defeat, Lord. Sometimes

harder for the sense that for whatever
reason, so few seem to understand or
care. You comfort us without question—
true to your word.

Most of all, Lord, you welcome us a friends—
as your children—when we are getting it
right and when we are inescapably clueless.
As surely predictable as our good
times and our bad times, you are always
true to your word.

BEYOND GOOD

You are beyond good, Lord.
Your ways stagger my imagination
yet inspire me to be like you.

You are patient with me
as a loving parent.
You stay with me
through tough times.

You correct me
with a tender hand.
You pursue me
when I wander off.

You comfort me
when my heart aches.
You calm me
when I am afraid.

You don't give up on me
when I don't get it right.
You provide beauty
when my soul is starving.

You speak clearly to me
when I am lonely.
You are kind to me
when I am irritable.

You cover me with wisdom
when I am foolish.
You are gentle with me
when I am fractured.

You forgive me

when I willfully disobey.
You love me
in spite of my bad habits.

And maybe best of all, Lord,
when I mess things up
horribly,
you always give me a
second chance.

Second Chance

Lord, we are amazed
at how you love us.
Not so much
in the beginning
when all is
fresh and new,
but in the middle
of our
sin,
rebellion,
arrogance,
disobedience
and
impudence—
you give us
a second chance.

And we are not always
so penitent, lord.
Sometimes we
keep right on doing
what we
want to do—
when we want,
what we want,
as we want.
Your loving voice
calls us to you,
but we have the
volume turned down.
Yet still we find
you give us
a second chance.

You tell us what you want,
what you expect,
how you want us
to live,
to love,
to care,
to provide,
to heal
and to follow you.
We listen when we
want to.
We obey when we
feel like it.
How can it be?
You give us
a second chance.

Just when we think
you will smash us
with your hammer
of justice
and stop us
dead still
in our tracks—
as we deserve,
we know!—
we see a light break,
and we feel the
fresh breeze
of your love
as you pour out
your grace and give us
a second chance.

I Won't Take Less

How much do I owe you, Lord, for all
you've done for me? For seeing me through the
hard times and messes I've made. For picking me up
again and again and cleaning me up. For unspeakable
comfort during times when I hurt. And courage to
carry on when I couldn't see the path. For a second
chance. A fresh start. A clean slate. A new heart.
Dare I ask the price for all this?

And how much do I owe you, Lord, for cool breezes,
snowy mountains, flowers, seas and majestic
storms? For friendships. And books. For healing
and security. For family. Income. Insights. Peace.
For music and art. Delicious food. Fun excursions.
Challenging conversations. Good wine and funny songs.
For poetry and films. Oh, how you have poured it out
on me, Lord. Do I really want to see a final bill?

Oh, how much do I owe you, Lord, for the hope of
heaven? For assurance of reunion with friends and family. For
salvation and redemption. For being your precious,
special child. For knowing you love me enough
to give your son, your self, to make me whole
and clean and pure. Just tell me, Lord, and I'll
pay whatever price you demand. Oh, thank you, Lord.
I hear you say *I won't take less than your love.*

Where Would We Be?

When the bottom drops out
of our world
and we feel the earth
give way beneath us;
When light is displaced
by utter darkness
and we sense the danger
all around us;
When the known fades into
the unknown
and we cannot see the path
ahead;
Then, Lord, then we
marvel that through it all
you have been with us,
right by our side.

And we wonder where
would we be
without you?

When our families
get all strange
and we see and hear
things that bewilder us;
when our jobs become
taskmasters
and we gasp for breath
against the pressure;
when change bursts in
without being announced
and demands a
new agenda;

Then Lord, then we
know that in your
quiet way, you have
walked every step with us.

And we wonder where
would we be
without you?

When our failures get
bigger than the blunders of others
and we are convicted
of our own sin;
When loss becomes an
ache
and we can't imagine
how we might survive;
When aging gets personal
and vicious
and we fill up with resentment
over declining faculties;
Then Lord, then we
understand that you
made us, you know us
and you love us through it all.

And we wonder where
would we be
without you?

Regress

Lord, we get hurt and offended when we
don't get our way. When we are overlooked, over-ruled,
out-voted or even out-maneuvered. And our hurt
feelings lead to a kind of craziness which abandons
judgment and wisdom in favor of

self-defense. And ultimately vengeance. How
quickly we can regress to perfected adolescent
thinking. How sharp our words can become. How
critical our thinking…condemning all others while
remaining blind to our own rage. We can

transform into surly, mean and foolish
children. And most often we would perish
in our vile state without the prompt action
and wise words offered by someone you
send. Action and words that save us. From

making total fools of ourselves. From wreaking
havoc on ourselves, our enemies, our innocent
friends, our family, our business, our church. For
those disguised angels we give you thanks. And
ask that you might even use us for that healing mission.

Confession and Forgiveness

We Confess

How mysterious the words seem to us, Lord, that we
should love you with all our
heart
soul
strength.
That seems like a mighty big order—
too big, in fact, for how we actually feel
most days. Yet there it is. Central to Israel's
life of faith and heralded by Jesus as
the most important thing we can do.
So here we are
asking for help
to get started.

Where do we begin, Lord? How should we approach
this mountainous challenge—this loving you best?
Do we even dare attempt it?
For something in us cries out for change
deep inside us before we can even get started.
In the hallowed center of our hearts we know
something big will be required of us.
Some painful change.
Some frightening rearrangement.
Some letting go.
Some giving up our right to be big
in our own eyes.
Some clear vision of who
and what we really are.

Telling the truth to you about ourselves—
which we fervently avoid—
means first admitting the truth
about ourselves
to ourselves.

And so, Lord, with but little real courage we take
the leap of reality and confess that
you are God. We confess we haven't acted like
we believe it. Help our unbelief.
We confess we have sinned against you
in thought
word
deed—
by what we have done,
and by what we have left undone.
We have not loved you with our whole heart;
we have not loved our neighbors as ourselves.
We are truly sorry
and we humbly repent.
For the sake of your son Jesus Christ
have mercy on us and forgive us;
that we may delight in your will,
and walk in your ways
to the glory of your name.

Looks Like Compassion

I'm most amazed, O Lord, when your grace looks like compassion. When you look me over, see what I've been through, know how nearly out of life I am, and you love me...like me...all the same. Someone told me once that I would have to be good, look good, live some perfect life for you to take any notice of me at all. What a tragedy of misinformation. What a waste of

time. And what an unthinkable affront to you. To think I could clean myself up sufficiently to merit your favor. That I could earn your affection by rule-keeping and right-living. As if you couldn't—wouldn't—see right through that kind of religious charade. As if there would ever be sufficient cleaning up to look good in your sight. It was almost a perfect formula for not

needing you at all if I could heal myself, forgive myself, save myself. But oh how you have shown me, Lord, oh how clearly you have let me see that my best salvation efforts are only a joke. So now I'm going to be as brave as I can be and say, *Here I am, Lord. Sinful through and through. Filthy from many falling downs. Wounded by many failures. Totally depending on your amazing grace that looks like compassion.*

Come Home

I hear your voice in the breeze, Lord. Whispering *Come Home. Come Home.* That plea takes me by surprise. Unnerves me. Makes me wonder how I got this far away. How I got in this shape. How things went so wrong. But here I am. Out of bright ideas. Out of luck. Out of strength. Wondering if I come home, will I find mercy? Will you even recognize me? Will you like me any more?

Come Home. Please come home. I feel the pull of your longing. *You are loved. Always. I'll pay the price. I'll bear the shame. You will be received as my precious child.* Your offer of grace amazes me. *I've been looking for you. Waiting. Hoping. My heart hurt every hour you were away. Come home. Come home. Let me sing over you.* And I see you running to meet

me. You? Running to find me? Me? And when I see you—holy, good, true, forgiving— only then do I know how ragged I must look. How beat up I am. How weak. How hungry. Then, only then, Lord, does my arrogance melt. And I see how outrageous my plan has been to save myself. To work my way into your favor. I feel the power of your *Come home.*

Feed Us

How hungry we get after leaving home, Lord. Oh, it's tolerable for a while because we have our minds made up and our jaw set. We tell ourselves there's nothing at all to fear—we simply need to stay focused on the goal, work hard, look good and keep our wits about us. The props we drag along to make us feel good about ourselves—oh! how important *that* is—too soon turn into dead weights we would leave beside

the path if we had any real courage. But our courage fades as our hunger grows. So we quicken our pace to put some distance between ourselves and you, thinking that any day we will arrive at whatever place it is we imagine can our fill our needs. No offense, Lord, but sometimes we feel we really need to make it on our own, provide for ourselves and be grown up at last.

But the hunger deepens and seeps into all our empty places like sand. Weighing us down and sapping our strength. Until the journey is no fun any more. The bright destination becomes only a mirage. Our path becomes too steep with the weight of all the heavy help we've thought to depend on. Until finally we can't go on any further. That's when we lay it all down and cry to you, *O Lord. Save us. Feed us.*

Gentle Shepherd

O Lord Jesus, Gentle Shepherd, how many times and
in so many ways have we wandered away from the
good, the beautiful, the nourishing, the secure,
the simple and you to follow after our own deluded idea
of greener pastures. Places and
adventures and prizes that dazzle and blind us
to the true worth of paths and pastures you
would lead us beside.

And how often we look up to see we are lost.
Stranded in isolation. Suddenly afraid. Not sure
which way to turn. Surrounded by enemies real and
imagined. Knowing too late that what glittered
was fool's gold after all. Not satisfying. No longer
even tempting or desirable. But hard, harsh,
garish and terrifying. And cowering in wastelands
of our own choosing, we cry out and wonder

what shall become of us? How will we ever be
found? Will we ever find our way home? Can
we hope for rescue? For deliverance? For the
ache deep inside to go away—even for a little
while? And just when, to all our longings—all
our questions—our answer comes slamming down
with loud finality: *NO! YOU ARE FINISHED!* Just then
we feel your arms lift us up into the brilliant light of hope.

Dirty Little Secrets

Our sins are forgiven and covered because of your generous grace, o Lord our God. Because of Jesus we stand pure in your sight. What a wonder. Certainly not because we are good, but in spite of our being bad. In spite of our dirty little secrets.

We confess we are more fearful of our secret sins being discovered by some other. Some really good person, maybe. How horrified we would be for public light to shine on our hidden attitudes and actions. Yet you, Lord, you know all along.

Forgive us for taking your forgiving grace so lightly. Lead us in paths of righteousness, Lord, so we may relax our defenses, show ourselves to each other as we really are and throw ourselves hourly on your mercy. Confident in your approval.

You Set the Standard

What a wonder that you accept us when we are
so unacceptable. Love us even as we are unlovable.
Rescue us when all others have given up. Save us
when we are beyond hope. Thank you, Lord, for
this greatest of all blessings. You set the
standard and call us to live it and pass it on.

We confess we haven't followed your lead,
your example, your plea, your command
to accept and honor each other and each
one we meet in the same manner.
For no other reason than that each is
made in your image. Each one is your

child. Forgive us, Lord. Please forgive us and
rescue us from our tarnished prejudices. How
we savor feeling superior because of your
beautiful grace. Lead us on a better path, Lord. Soften
our hearts so we may walk in the
Spirit and offer to all men and women love and respect.

TRUST

We Hear You

We hear you calling us, Lord.
On good days we hear you loud and clear.
And even on bad days the world's siren song
never completely drowns out your voice.
We hear you asking us to
follow you
trust you
honor you.
We hear you begging us to
seek you
find you
love you.
We hear you reminding us that you alone
are worthy of our
admiration
reverence
confidence.

We hear you, Lord.
And part of us wants more than anything
to find comfort and encouragement
in your voice, and to
respond to you with the best that we
have and are.
Part of us longs for the place of rest
your call offers.
Part of us knows that life
in you
would be the very best
of all possibilities.

We hear you, Lord.
But part of us finds it hard to let go

of our own ambitions
and the solutions we have
figured out for ourselves.
Part of us demands that we keep
trusting in ourselves
or at least in what
we can see and touch.

Cut through our layers of defense, Lord. Our
defiance
arrogance
self-sufficiency
greed
and all the things in us that keep telling us
to ignore your call.

Go to work on us, Lord.
In us.
Remake us in your image
so we can love you first and best.

We hear you calling us, Lord.
Help us, please,
to listen.

Choices

It seems, Lord, that your great men and women of faith
have always, sooner or later, been faced
with choices. Some of them really tough
choices that involved
life or death
good or evil
right or wrong
strength or weakness.
Or maybe what to say
or not to say
or what to do
or not to do
or how to get a thing done
or which path to travel
or maybe even, sometimes, what it really
means to trust you.
My friend is just now wrestling with some choices, or
maybe better said, with a choice. So this prayer, Lord,
is about him
and for him.
You've heard some of this stuff before from me, Lord, but
I hope you don't mind my bringing it up again.

What I want to ask starts with the decision that he
is facing: will you please empower him with the strength
of your Spirit to see what he needs to see,
go where he needs to go,
do what he needs to do
and be what he needs to be?
And what I really mean by that, Lord, is will you somehow
let him know what those needs are? Will you
show him, instruct him
where he needs to go

what he needs to do
and what he needs to be?
And then will you anoint all that with your presence in
a way that he can very really sense, and
hold on to
and depend on
as being what you want for him, what you
will for him?

I know that's asking a very special favor, Lord. But
somehow I'm completely confident that you know
what I'm asking for and
that you will grant it.

And then there's something else I'm asking for—
for this friend. Lord, will you lend him the light of your
encouragement so that
whatever he does
wherever he goes
and in whatever circumstance
or place
or position
or job
or predicament
he finds himself in
he will know beyond any doubt
that you are with him
and that the strength of your mighty arm
will hold him and protect him?
But above all that, Lord, I ask that you grant him
an extra measure of faith
so he can trust you completely
and totally and choose you
and faithfulness to you
and loyalty to you
first and beyond all else.

O Sovereign Lord

What might my life have been like up to
now, Lord, if I had early learned
you were really in control?
Oh, I've known it in theory, of course.
The Bible and all those sermons
heard and spoken confirmed your
right to rule. But I'm not so sure
I ever really let it sink into my way
of thinking that you are not
simply powerful—but
all-powerful.

How might I have received and
responded to your promises, Lord,
if I had understood who it was
making the promises. I know
too well all about the promises
we make to each other in this
life; some are weighty enough
to be counted on; most are light as
air and dissipate in a moment of
neglect. Yours are backed up by heavenly
authority. Yours are worth trusting.
But I think what scares me most, Lord,
is how I've spoken to you when
things weren't going my way. I've
challenged. I've protested. I've
accused. I've stormed and howled
about how unfair you have been to
allow some things to happen to me.
I'm pretty sure I've spoken to you as if
you were my irresponsible servant who forgot
to secure my comfort instead of as the Lord

of the universe.

Forgive me for getting it so wrong, Lord.
For putting my confidence in anyone
but you. And especially for trusting
in myself as if I were in charge.
Please let me start over.
Teach me what it means to
revere you and trust you
and follow you and learn from you
and depend on you. Form yourself in me
so that I can with confidence address you as
O Sovereign Lord.

Whenever You're Ready

I come from a long line of workers, Lord.
If there was a job to be done
you could count on us!
Work for the night is coming
has been our theme song.
We'll work till Jesus comes and
To the Work, to the Work!
we sang
with gusto.
Agendas, plans, campaigns,
meetings, minutes,
budgets and bylaws
have always made us happy.
We've had lists of things to do,
some for us
and some for you.
And we've been known to say,
OK, Lord—
whenever you're ready!

We need this building, Lord—
whenever you're ready!
We need this program, Lord—
whenever you're ready!
We need this recovery, Lord—
whenever you're ready!
We need this renewal, Lord—
whenever you're ready!
We need this expansion, Lord—
whenever you're ready!

We need this conversion, Lord—
whenever you're ready!
We need this healing, Lord—
whenever you're ready!
We need this blessing, Lord—
whenever you're ready!
We need to get this done, Lord—
whenever you're ready!

Truth is, Lord, you've kept us
waiting.
You've been slow to
give us what we want.
You've been negligent in
doing the things on
the lists we've given
to you.
And our sensibilities
have been offended.
Our feelings have been
hurt
because, haven't we
made it perfectly
clear what we
need from you?
And we've always humbly
said—whenever you're ready!

What's that you say, Lord?
Our work wears you out?
Our agendas leave you out?
Our budgets and lists,
our meetings and minutes,

our bylaws and plans
are beside the point?
Then dare we ask, Lord,
at this late date,
what it is you want?
And from the thunder
and sunshine,
from Torah, Psalms and
Gospels
we hear at last
your sweet voice say,
I have it all for you, children—
whenever you're ready.

My peace is yours—
whenever you're ready.
My joy is yours—
whenever you're ready.
My grace is yours—
whenever you're ready.
My righteousness is yours—
whenever you're ready.
My abundance is yours—
whenever you're ready.
My cleansing is yours—
whenever you're ready.
My healing is yours—
whenever you're ready.
My salvation is yours—
whenever you're ready.
My blessing is yours—
whenever you're ready.

Teach Us To Pray

Lord, we've been carefully trained
not to ask you for too much.
Our daily bread was
to be enough.
We weren't supposed
to want for more than
we already have.
Don't worry about clothes.
Don't fret about how you look.
Work hard.
Enjoy what little you have.
Don't be greedy.
You'll have a mansion
in heaven someday.
These were our lessons from
earliest childhood.

Somewhere along the way, Lord,
we became the providers
and you became
the recipient.
We give you our
service,
tithes,
allegiance,
faith,
praise,
time,
energy
and adoration;
You take it all in
and decide if it is

good enough.
Meanwhile, we began to believe, Lord,
that all we have
comes from our hand,
not yours.
And so, quite naturally,
we began to ask you
to bless
our labors,
our efforts,
our work
and our service
in an effort to somehow
keep you around
while we went about
doing what
needed to be done.

Providing for ourselves
what needed providing;
giving to ourselves
what needed giving;
securing for ourselves
what needed securing;
Saving for ourselves
what needed saving.
Somehow forgetting, Lord,
that you are
the provider,
the giver,
the one who secures
and the one who saves.
Forgive our preposterous
arrogance, Lord. Forgive us.

Give us more, Lord.
Give us more.
More money to feed more hungry.
More clothes to warm more cold.
More resources to spread the gospel.
More facilities to edify the church.
More venues to do good.
More words to encourage the hopeless.
More strength to lift the fallen.
More grace to forgive the sinner.
More time to walk with you.
More energy to right wrongs.
Give us more, Lord.
Give us more.
Above all, give us the humility to
see you, once more, as the giver.

And be with us, Lord.
Every step of the way.
Don't leave us alone.
Don't abandon us.
Don't forsake us.
Walk with us.
Abide with us.
Hold our hand.
Shed light on our path.
Show us the way.
Guide us.
Help us see.
Give us words.
Be our strength.
Let us lean on you.
And deliver us from evil, Lord.

Keep us out of harm's way.

Protect us from the evil one.
Guard our path.
Warn us away from temptation.
Rescue us, as only you can,
from all that would
bring us to ruin.
Take care of us.
Lead us in paths of
righteousness.
Keep us pure.
Keep us safe.
Watch over us.
Look out for us.
Call us by name.

Bless us, Lord.
Richly bless us.
Provide for us, Lord.
Bountifully provide for us.
Be with us, Lord.
Keep your hand always on us.
Deliver us from evil, Lord.
Keep us from all harm.
For thine is the
kingdom
and the
power
and the
glory
for ever
and ever.

Sing Over Us

We want to love our children well, Lord.
We want to
hold them close,
hold them loosely,
celebrate their victories,
forgive their waywardness,
overlook their mistakes,
glory in their success,
honor their needs
and nurture
the nature
you gave them.

We want to guide our children well, Lord.
We want to
help them make good choices,
show them how to face challenges,
lead them to love you,
demonstrate for them how to keep trying,
train them to respect others,
coach them to play fair,
teach them to forgive
and encourage them
to live up to
their potential.

We want to love them, Lord,
just as you love us—
unconditionally.
We want to guide them
just as you guide us—
gently and surely.

We want to do these things, Lord,

but, oh how hard it is.
We want to do it right, Lord,
but how often we mess it up.
We argue when we should listen.
We judge when we should forgive.
We scold when we should comfort.
And we hold a grudge
when we should
light a torch.

Teach us again, Lord,
how we should be
and what we should say.
Show us again, Lord,
what love looks like
and how guidance feels.

Bring us again, Lord,
to the place where
you are the Father
and we are your children.
Remind us how you
rejoice in us.
Quiet us with
your
presence.
Come, Lord,
sing over us.

Speak to Me

Lord, I do want you to
speak to me
and tell me
what's on your mind,

as long as what you

have to say
won't
upset me,
make me uncomfortable,
demand too much
or create much of a disturbance;

as long as what you
have to say
won't
cost me anything,
be an inconvenience,
require any changes
or force me to look too closely
at myself;

as long as what you
have to say
won't
challenge me to think too hard,
interfere with my plans,
hurt my feelings
or contradict what I already know.

I'm embarrassed to admit this, Lord—
but it's the truth.
So, before you
speak to me
and tell me
what's on your mind—
you can see
I'm not ready—
you will probably have to
shake me up
and get my attention.

You will have to change me, Lord,
or I'll have to
change myself—
I'm not really sure
just how this works.

Change my mind, Lord—
give me a new one.
Change my disposition, Lord—
give me a new one.
Change my value system, Lord—
give me a new one.
Change my will, Lord—
give me a new one.
Change my name, Lord—
give me a new one.

Then, whenever you're ready, Lord,
speak to me
and tell me
what's on your mind.

You Are My Shield

When we least expect it, Lord,
when we are not looking,
not anticipating
anything to come along
that might hurt us,
that might blow us off course
that might knock us off our feet;

When we have the feeling
that everything
is going
pretty much OK;

When we feel
secure,
prepared,
experienced,
strong
and confident;

From out of nowhere, it seems,
come
surprises,
losses, failures,
heartbreaks,
challenges and
discouragements.

And our sense of security
evaporates like a mist.
Our well-laid plans
unravel before our eyes.
Our strength ebbs.
Our hope wanes.

Ray Hardin

Our courage falters.

And we see our desperate condition
for exactly what it is—
we are
unprotected,
unprepared,
vulnerable and
defenseless.

Then it is, Lord, then it is
we feel your hand
lift us up,
straighten us out,
clean us off.

Then it is, Lord,
the blinding light of sorrow
softens.
For then it is, Lord,
we find ourselves
beneath the shadow
of your shield.

For should everything
around us change,
you, oh Lord,
remain the same.
You are a
shield
about
us.
You lift
our heads.

Hallelujah!

Teach Me to Praise

There is something in me that
wants to praise you, Lord.
Some urge I didn't put there.
Some longing I can't name that
worries my well-being and
unbalances my fragile stability
until it gets what it demands.
Relentless, it howls and whispers
your name, wanting—needing—
an echo.

Cares and concerns conspire to
quiet it with sheer force of
weight. Neglect and abuse join
hands to cool its heat of urgency, hoping
sufficient time elapsed will dull
the sharp edge of need to groan,
whisper, speak, sing,
shout some expression
of praise.

But nothing can totally extinguish
its flame. Pressed in on all sides
by the darkness of my choices—some
made defiantly, some heedlessly,
some stupidly—reduced at
times to the smallest flicker, it
burns on as an eternal demand
for the oxygen of my spirit
to praise.

Dig deep into my being, Lord, down to that
part of me that looks most like you.
Unearth that rare essence of yourself—that
urge, that heat, that sword, that flame,

that endless need I so often
deny and perennially overlook—and
breathe life into it—into
me—once more so I
can praise.

Light of the World

How dark the earth before light.
no shadow
no glow
no illumination
no hope
What part of God's nature
loved and laughed
in the darkness?
What spark of creativity said
enough is enough?
In darkness I can see
and feel
and experience
and love
and laugh
and create.
Spirit needs no light.
But you, oh man of limits,
will require material
comfort for your flesh,
challenge for your mind
and light for your eyes.
So be it then.
Let there be light.
And all three laughed
out loud when there was
light.
Good, said Father.
Brilliant, said Spirit.
It is like me, said Son.

Ray Hardin

How dark, how dark
just before the
light of the world.

Praise to the Lord

Lord, we praise you right now.
Not because everything is perfect—
or even anything like we would have it be—
but because you deserve our praise.
And because when we start
praising you
recognizing you
appreciating you
honoring you
remembering you
the weight is lifted from our self-imposed
task of making everything turn out right.

We confess that we are addicted to
arranging good endings and positive results—
even when we are most clueless how to do it—
because we have been carefully taught
to be responsible for every possible
turn of events
potential outcome
dangerous consequence
mysterious conclusion
ambivalent reaction
instead of submitting to you and learning
to trust your ability to take care of all circumstances.

So we praise you Lord while asking above
all things that you would please open our
eyes to the eternal, changeless truth
that you are in charge of us—

all we are and all we do—
and that we can relax in the
certain knowledge that in your hands
all is well.

Cultish Tightness

I have come to a place of contrived peace with
my church tradition, Lord. How I admire the simple
faith in your power to unify all believers. And how I
grieve over those primary principles having been twisted
into ugly and unforgiving tests of faith and fellowship. You were
there watching as it unfolded into a cultish tightness
never intended by its crafters. Did you wince, as I now do

upon reflecting what might have been? And about what now
challenges us? Forgive my ancestors, Lord, for getting it wrong.
And us, also, my sovereign,
please forgive us for having mutely endured these
decades of mutilation of that which began no nobly: *we
shall stand firm and resolute. And defend to the death the
possibility—the reality—of the unity of all believers. We
shall not—ever!—bind opinions regarding matters of reflection upon*

*any people. Any where. At any time. And we shall, with your
help, grow into the image of Jesus who lived, thought, breathed
and taught the deepest, most mature level of understanding of your
heart. That you, O Lord our God, want and insist—above all
else, that we should be of one mind, unified, bonded, steadfastly
devoted to each other in the singular ambition of presenting through our
broken lives the beauty of your wholeness and holiness for all to see.*

Who Do You Say?

It's too easy for me to coast along and not
think too often about who you are, Lord.
There's so much to *do*, for one thing.
And, as you know, much of what I'm doing
these days is for you, after all. the number of
projects I'm involved in here at church seems to
grow without my being real sure of when I said *yes*.

Oh, I've got it pretty well settled in my mind that
you are the one, great and true God. You are the
maker of it all. The life-giver to it all. You are in
charge of it all. And being confident in that goes a
long way in keeping me pretty calm and steady.
But I wonder if you were to step into my path
right now and ask me who you are—well, what would I say?

Would I answer *you are good*? Which, of course, you are.
Or maybe *all-powerful*. Or *all-knowing*. Or *you are
the great provider*. Or *you are the one who loves me*.
Or maybe I'd say *well everyone thinks you are
wonderful, Lord! Really wonderful!* But would I
rise to the occasion and answer your question *who do
you say that I am?* with *you are the Lord of my life?*

Honor

I'm just now, Lord, beginning to understand your
plan. Rather late in life, I know. I'm sorry it took
me so long to believe you've always had my best
interest in mind when you prompt me to do some
things that don't come so naturally. And its
not that I thought your ideas were bad. I just had
a hard time believing you meant *me* and not someone else.

So I concluded that I didn't need to try too hard to
honor anyone so long as I didn't blatantly dishonor.
Oh, you know, Lord, I didn't get *that* right a lot of times. But
when I did, I felt pretty good about it. Because I've had
plenty of chances to tear someone down, but remembered,
just in time, to let it go. You might say I built a system
of goodness based on what I didn't do. On refraining.

Which must look pretty pathetic to you since you
have always seemed more interested in what I do
than in what I don't do. And that untold number of times
I could have—should have—given honor but didn't
is a loud testimony to just how wrong I've been.
So please forgive me, Lord, for not doing what you
asked me to do. And for substituting my plan for yours.
And given a fresh start, I promise, Lord, that I
will look for ways to build someone up. To
say an encouraging word. To see and fill a need.
To praise and commend. To congratulate. To
rejoice in success. To find something good and
positive and beautiful in everyone and every thing
you put on my path. To learn at last to honor.

You Have Been Good

These days of ours, Lord, are
sometimes hard.
We struggle with deadlines;
we worry about money;
we mourn losses;
we battle aging and
we wonder if we are
doing life even
halfway right.

And our days gone by, Lord,
sometimes hang around
like dangerous shadows
threatening to
remind us,
frighten us,
discourage us,
undo us and
make us wonder
if yesterday's decisions
were made even
halfway right.

But our days ahead, Lord, often
make us tremble
as we face
uncertainty,
unknown challenges,
mysterious obstacles and
riddles to solve for
which we feel
unprepared.

We wonder if we shall
manage our future even
halfway right.

Our collective dilemma, Lord, is
weakness.
Our universal need is
deliverance.
Our spiritual challenge is
unbelief.
Our social danger is
isolation, and
our intellectual problem is
arrogance.

How shall we deal with
our present,
our past,
our future and
our inadequacy
without
you?

Lift us up, Lord, to a new
level of awareness
and appreciation
for who you are
and how you have
ever been
faithful,
good,
steadfast,
merciful,
unchanging,

upright,
holy,
strong and
loving
for all generations.

Call My Name

What was that, Lord? Did you just call
my name? Yes? You did? And
you have been calling me all this time?
How could I have missed that, Lord?
I've been howling in the night—begging to
hear something from you.

What was that, Lord? You've been waiting for
a moment of silence? A brief pause? For
me to be quiet enough to hear your voice?
And here I thought all along your call would
be so loud and clear I could not miss it.
I wasn't listening for a whisper.

What was that, Lord? You have a plan
for me? For me? Something no one else can
do but me? Something really special?
Oh! I guess I'm surprised by that. I've
never seen myself doing anything important.
I just wanted to know you were there.

What was that, Lord? You've known
me since when? Really? Since before time
began? You've planned and seen my whole life already?
I can't understand how that's possible, Lord.
But if you say so, I'll try to imagine it.
Just imagine! No one here understands me like that.

What was that, Lord? You love me for being me? You
do? You love me just as much when I listen
as when I ignore you or tune you out?
I guess I always figured you loved me when
I'm being good. But I've been pretty sure
you wouldn't—couldn't love me all the rest of the time.

What was that, Lord? You have a plan for others? A
plan that involves me? You want me to be an
example that someone else will want to follow?
Oh, Lord! I'm not so sure about this. I don't
think it may be such a good idea to let anyone
else depend on my example—my life.

What was that, Lord? You've got it figured out? You
do? All you want me to do is listen? And
follow you wherever you lead me?
OK, Lord. But that's pretty scary. After all, here I've
been missing your call. And something tells
me I've been missing some other things, too.

What was that, Lord? You know I haven't been
listening? You know
I'm not good and strong?
Your strength is all I need to be all you expect from me?
Well, frankly, Lord, that's a huge relief. And a new
way of looking at things for me. I'll remember
what you've said. But...just in case...will you call my name again?

OUTWARD

What Are They Doing Here?

Where are you going with this, Lord? You're really making me nervous here. Suggesting within a clever story that we are all the same. That we all get the same treatment. No matter what. Are you serious? You want me to come in and party with you and with... *them*? All I can think of is, *What are they doing here?* I thought this was a rather exclusive club with rights and privileges, you know? A place that

protected us from having to deal with people like them. Afforded us some level of privacy. And insured a proper balance of propriety. After all, Lord, you must surely understand! Membership has its advantages! What value are we supposed to see in a kingdom community that you apparently think should be open to the weak, the unemployed, the hopeless, helpless, homeless? The addicted, the

convicted, the rebellious. Really, Jesus! They are not like us! These doctrinally unsound who can't even get worship and salvation issues right. They should know better. And what are we to think of the ones who are certainly too old, too young, too powerful, too rich? Democrats, gays, uneducated, divorced, single? They make me nervous, Lord. They really do. They should be more like me. I really can't come in as long as they're in there.

One of us is simply going to have to change our viewpoint about who is in and who is out.

Blind Eye

Some days I am ready to serve others, Lord. Alert to needs—huge or small, grand or humble, demanding or simple—something in me says yes with little hesitation, or none at all. And not counting the cost to myself I wade into pools of need with sleeves rolled up and simply go to work doing what is there to do. It isn't so much like setting out to serve as it is following an instinct, which later, if I think about

it, I figure comes from you. But other times, Lord, find me not seeing anyone else's needs, blind to any but my own. Or thinking too much, trying to figure out if I should get involved, if I should take the risk, if I should exert the energy, spend the time or make the investment. Even questioning whether the person in need has put himself there through some stupid self-indulgence. Wondering if by helping I may be enabling some self-destructive

behavior that should be owned up to, not excused or overlooked. O, Jesus, suffering servant and my daily helper, please come to my rescue and deliver me from thinking too much, judging too harshly, excusing myself to easily while glibly justifying my blind eye and hard heart. Give me more of the days when I serve without thinking and less of those which focus too much on me. Cleanse my heart and empower my vision to see you as I serve.

Who is My Neighbor?

As the giver of all things, Lord,
are you the one who
keeps putting these people in my path?
Am I supposed to see them
as a gift from you
instead of a bother
like I'm inclined to do?
Are they like clues to help me
learn to love you best?
Are they the neighbor I'm
supposed to love like
I love myself?

I would have preferred
a different gift, Lord.
Why not give me instead
a lofty cathedral
to inspire me?
a mountain view
to awe me?
a still lake
to quiet me?
I nearly always come
to you
in those places.

And you know how busy I am, Lord.
Busy doing church work.
Busy making a living.
Busy caring for my family.
Busy writing these lessons.
Busy trying to keep up
with everything.

And these gifts that you
keep putting in my path
always seem to need something
just when
I am at my limit.

Just when I'm running late.
Just when I'm nearly overwhelmed.
Just when I'm feeling impatient.
Just when I'm exhausted
or worried
sad
perplexed
discouraged
or just plain fed up
with trying to fit
one more thing into
my schedule.
And to tell you the truth, Lord,
some of these gifts of yours
I'd just as soon not
have to deal with.
I don't know what to say.
I can't solve their problem.
I've heard it all before.
They seem never to get any better.
And, really, Lord,
some of them
truly do
irritate me.

So, as with all your gifts, Lord,
I need your help
knowing what to do with these
needy ones you keep putting
in my path.

Start with me, Lord.
Cleanse my heart so that I can
love you best.
Heal my blindness so that I can
see your beauty
in every stranger
who begs to be my neighbor.

Swallow Us, Lord

We run away from your grace
that wants to bless everyone, Lord;
from your compassion
that wants to save
even our enemies.

While saying, even out loud,
that we honor faith and grace
above all else, there are
some people we really
want to see punished.

Soften our hearts, Lord,
toward our enemies—
people who are different from us
or who don't treat us very well.
Overrule our judgment.

Because we would like
to hold a grudge.
It tastes so good to
feel better than others because
we have you and they have nothing.

Frankly, Lord, we like it that way. After all,
who will we call "those others"
if all
those others
end up belonging to you?

We would really like to see
them suffer, Lord.

Ray Hardin

We really want you to
punish them. Give them justice.
Give us mercy.

So we run away from you and
from our job of holding up the light
of your grace.
We run so we might stop
hearing your voice.

Yet even as we wear ourselves out
running from your presence,
we feel your hot breath on our neck
as you run after us.
Oh, God, you will not let us go.

So go ahead Lord,
swallow us.
Prepare whatever rescue
might stop us
from running away.

Use whatever miracle
you need to get our attention,
slow us down
melt our heart
and bring us back to you.

Teach us again, Lord,
the sweet message we heard
at first: your love, your grace,
your giving, your forgiving
is for everyone.

Objects of Honor

I wonder, Lord, how the church—in its very
early days—received this instruction. This demand,
actually, to live into a principle of taking care of others.
Were they distressed to think they must submit to
others, honor others, be devoted to others and help bear
with each other? Did it sound strange and new to them?
Frankly, Lord, I wonder if they got it. I wonder if they

lived it. And how, Lord, shall we hear these words?
Are they gentle encouragement? Urgent reminders?
Solemn commands? Do they whisper or shout?
Can we get some other things figured out first, or
do these principles of life take precedence over
heavier questions? What would our days look
like if we learned these lessons? And what might we

look like to our culture outside the church if we really
started treating each other as objects of honor and
worth? As opportunity to serve instead of irritants
to avoid? Show us the simplicity of these invitations,
Lord, and the beauty of living in ways that
reflect your thorough, deep goodness. Lead us into
paths of following Jesus with pure hearts and open hands.

Spiritual Leverage

O God of heaven, earth and our hearts, pry us loose from the callous lethargy that too often disrupts intent and inhibits action. We see needs, small and large, in nearly everyone we meet. We sometimes even feel your Spirit urging us to speak a word,

offer a touch, make a visit, bear a gift or carry a load. But our defenses are well-rehearsed and powerful. And too often we give ourselves credit for recognizing the need, seeing what we might do to help, even as

we stop short of actually taking any action. And so need and service both fade away untended, unanswered, unfulfilled. Hearts remain troubled, burdens remain heavy. Hands remain empty, neither giver or receiver able to connect in your Name.

So we ask now for an extra measure of spiritual leverage to pry us loose from safe mornings, fear timidity and reserve. Fill us up with your compassion and nudge us forward so that, forgetting ourselves, we may speak, touch, visit, and gift those in need we

meet daily. Open our eyes to ones who are hurting. Sharpen our hearing as we listen for silent cries for help. Show us, however you choose, what we may do and the right way to do it. And deliver us from waiting any longer to so live that your Kingdom may appear.

Whispered Blessing

O God heaven and earth, how we wish for
a second chance. Some way to undo or get
beyond the mess we've made of things. Or the
mess someone else has made that troubles us
as much as them. And so we breath out—

barely audible—our *would that, how I
wish* or *if only.* And though sometimes those little
prayers are for others, most often they are for
ourselves. Reviewing our life with regret and the weight
of sorrow, we wish things were different. Better.

Maybe more like they once were—back when. Or
more like we would have them be. Careers. Husband.
Wife. Health. Children. Finances. *would that.
How I wish. If only.* Our soft prayers
ricochet off heaven's grace and come back to us

with a question: what would your world look like
if your whispered prayers for yourself got somehow
transformed into whispered blessings for others?
Would they make any difference? Would they change
anything? Could they open the way for a second chance?

Guarded Looks

O Lord our God we are surrounded by young and
old and all in between who are stuck in the quicksand
of deprivation and need. No jobs, or at best unreliable and
intermittent revenue. No training or education. Few skills. And
little understanding of how things work or how they can get

on with living productively. We would move, O Lord, from
caring only about ourselves to caring for these others. We
want to feel a concern for these who have little, need
much and harbor small hope for anything getting
better. Or things changing much. They furtively

take guarded looks at our outrageous, unprecedented
wealth and wonder what went wrong in their world.
Why are all doors closed and why is there no work,
no money, no training, no opportunity for education
and, so it seems to them, no one who cares? Lay on

our hearts, Lord, the future of these without secure
foundations, without families to protect and provide
for them, without resources and without any sense
that tomorrow may, indeed, be a better day. Inspire
us, Lord. Teach us. Lead us. Nudge us. In whatever

way you choose. Give us courage, daring, creativity
and energy to follow your call to become servants
in your world and not simply consumers. Open
our eyes. Sharpen our hearing. Soften our hearts. Toughen
our wills and strengthen our resolve. Please cultivate

us as your eyes, ears, hands and feet. Keep
remaking us in your image until we
hurt when we see these others hurt. Until we move
ourselves from passive comfort to areas and times
of awkward giving. And providing. And blessing.

GOD'S WILL

Did You Mean?

I get it, Lord. You want me to accept everyone. But did you mean the pushy, the bossy, the overbearing, the arrogant, the proud, the rude, the thoughtless, the hateful, the self-important, the name-dropper, the careless, the offensive, the critical, the judgmental, the insufferable? Did you want me to accept them,

also? I get it, Lord. You want me to accept everyone. But did you have in mind the negative, the self-pitying, the victim, the loser, the lazy, the under-achiever, the slacker, the drop-out, the no-show, the free-loader, the leech, the uninterested, the tuned-out, the accident-prone, the procrastinator? Did you actually want me to accept them, too?

I get it, Lord. You want me to accept everyone. But did you mean the drunk, the cheat, the liar, the glutton, the gossip, the complainer, the trouble-maker, the gay man, the lesbian, the ex-con, the untrustworthy? Did you really want me to accept them, too? Remind me, Lord, why is that? Oh. Because you accept me. Oh, Lord. Help me here.

More Like You

You O Lord are never careless. Your watchful
gaze somehow lingers on each of us. Your heart
stays full of care and concern for where we are,
how we're doing and what we are up to. Even
when we feel lost and not worth much, you see us
with eyes of love. And sometimes, Lord, knowing *that*
is about all that keeps us going. Because even in
those darkest hours when we think no one else

values us or cares much about us, we sense
and know that you still count us precious. Irreplaceable.
Unique. Priceless. Worthy. For that grace we
thank you. And in turn we love you back. We can't
help ourselves. We love you back. And give you our
hearts with our thanks. Sometimes for the
life of us we can't figure out why you think so much of
us, but knowing you do makes worthwhile

days of darkness and nights of fear. Breathe into us,
O Lord, some of that same sense of care. For ourselves,
for each other, for causes that matter, for lives broken
by disappointment, for the many around us who have
not yet lived the joy of knowing they are loved by you.
For the sad, the weak, the tired, the disillusioned,
the self-destructive and the tormented. Oh, yes, Lord,
give us some of your caring heart so we may be more like you.

Giving Way

I know deep down in my most honest
place that I will never figure out
this submitting to others thing until I learn to
submit to you. And you know me, Lord.
I've got to figure it out before I can start
putting it into practice. And you also know, Lord,
how much I want to have my own way.

Oh, I can rise to the occasion occasionally
when I must give way in order to
get along. I can roll out the words
No, Please! After you! Or *You may be
right about this.* Or even *Whatever you
think best.* But I confess: too often
my heart is not in it.

And too often I end up feeling heroic
after letting someone else have his way. Like
I've done some great courtesy which really
deserves to be recognized and appreciated. And
I'm pretty good at keeping score of the
number of time I've given in—especially to
someone who to my best reckoning should give in to me
at least every once in a while. But I'm
wandering away again from my real problem of
not having learned yet that when I submit myself to
you, Lord, it will be easier—I know it will—to
submit to someone else. And such a
little thing, really, not to have my way every time.
Especially if even once my giving way glorifies your name.

Devoted

O Lord, our God, why did you ask me to be
devoted to my fellow church members? Didn't
you know that some of them would be hard to get
along with? Insisting always on their own way?
Too ready to cast stones and jump to unworthy
conclusions? With prickly personalities that
bring out my worst instead of my best? Couldn't you

have taken that down a notch or two and suggested
instead that I do my best to tolerate them? Or
maybe to simply steer clear of them as a way to promote
peace? Didn't you know that some of them will hurt
my feelings, or say unkind words, or be so disagreeable
that what at times I really want to do is give them a dose of
their own medicine? A dig in kind? Or maybe an

occasional, intentional and obvious snub that would make me
feel better about having endured what they dish out on a
regular basis? Really, Lord, I think you have no idea
what a challenge this teaching can be for me. How it goes
against the grain. Or how I must strain to do it your way.
Until, that is, I see my sinful, rebellious self through your
eyes. Until I see your look that says to me, "I am devoted."

A Prophet's Voice

We do a better job of imagining what worship will look like in heaven than what it might be like in church, Lord. We like the idea of crowns being cast before you. Of a numberless choir singing *Holy! Holy! Holy!* We are not even all that uncomfortable with a trumpet or two in *that* setting. Or bowing down, come to think of it, since everyone else will be doing it, too.

It's church that stumps us. Contrary to our strongest resolve, we too often file into the worship center wondering *What are we in for today?* And *Will we sing any songs I know? Will it be so loud I can't think? Will I hear anything that makes any sense at all?* These fears leave someone else—anyone else—in charge of what we receive. And what we contribute.

Deliver back to us, Lord, a voice—a loud prophet's voice—that calls us to enter your presence as your church with awe. With reverence. With anticipation. With wonder. Make bold our own voice to cry *Today we want to hear a word from the Lord! Today we want to practice abandon in adoring you.* So maybe heaven won't come as such a shock.

Sweet Will of God

How sweet it is, Lord, when we find
ourselves in harmony
with what you want.
We enjoy ourselves when
you are pleased.
So we seek your will. We want
to know what you
want from us,
what you want us to be and do.
Speak, Lord, and we will obey.

Until what you seem to be telling us
simply does not line up
with what we believe
or what we need
or what we want
or how we thought things
might work out.
And then it seems the most
natural thing in the world to
think you simply must be wrong.

Then we wonder, Lord, if in fact
you may have lost your mind.
And when we suffer while loving you
as others prosper while
thumbing their nose at you,
it gets tough, Lord, in those still
quiet hours of reflection, to
believe we are on the right course,
that you want what is best for us
and that things really will turn out alright.

And sometimes, Lord, the pain gets

so big that we want to stop
hearing from you. So we run away
hoping the voices will be still.
Then, Lord, then please pursue us.
Come after us and find us where we
have hidden. Be gentle with us.
Rescue us.
Teach us.
Show us

that you are mercy and
your very nature is love.
Convince us again that
everything belongs to you
and that your ways are
good even when we don't understand.
Draw us again into wanting what you want,
loving what you love.
So we may live and die in
your sweet will.

One God

Blessed art thou, O Lord our God, King
of the universe. God of heaven and earth.
God of all. Over all. One God. Now and
forever. One God. And only one God. With,
it appears, three distinctive, representative

voices: the sovereign, holy God the father,
the mind of God incarnated in Jesus, and
the mysterious, ever-moving Spirit of God who
stops and starts where he sees best. Ever
intent upon our confidence, our instruction

and our comfort. Not to say, Lord, that we
have you all figured out. Though we try.
We come closest to accepting you by accepting
Jesus even though we don't really understand
what he meant much of the time. And we bristle

at your sovereign holiness more than we want to
admit. We sometimes find you arbitrary and hard
to reason with. But we genuinely do not get the
Spirit. Many of us were carefully taught not to
believe your Spirit is alive, well, present and
instrumental today. We are recovering. And
discovering again this enigmatic third dimension
who makes possible our renewal. Provides
sacred second chances for us to relax in your
care, born again as it were, into your eternal kingdom.

Intimate Love Letter

We say we want to hear from you, O Lord our God. How glorious it would be, we tell each other, if you sent us messages today. You know, like you used to do a long time ago. With maybe a trembling mountain or two, some bright

light. Or fire even. Better still, we think, to receive a personal up-close visit from an angel who knows everything we've been through and what's around the corner. If you should choose an angel, please remind her to tell us it's OK and

we don't have to be afraid. Although I'm not sure that reassurance would keep us from sheer terror. Or maybe a universal announcement addressed to all of us at the same time. Something like *Here's what I want you to do!* Or even a small

voice, whispering an intimate love letter from you to each of us individually. To tell us how we are to solve the big problems, how to work on the medium-sized ones and how to live with the little ones. Or perhaps a word of comfort, persuading us that you are still there and you still like us. O Lord, how helpful that would be! We Wait. We've waited a long time. With only one reservation: what if your message turned out to be something other than we expected or hoped for?